W0017887

Transforming Central Finance Agencies in Poor Countries

A Political Economy Approach

THE WORLD BANK
Washington, D.C.

Contents

Figures

Tables

Preface

This report presents the findings of a study of functions carried out by country Central Finance Agencies (CFAs) that was financed jointly by the Bank Netherlands Partnership Program (BNPP), the Korean Trust Fund (KTF) and the World Bank over a three-year period from July 2008 to mid-2011. The main outputs of the study comprise the present report, a set of ten country reports submitted to the national authorities and related "political economy" notes, and the dataset describing the organization and structure of CFAs in 55 countries. An earlier version of this synthesis report was provided to the Dutch authorities in June 2011.

It is expected that the findings of the study will be of interest to several audiences. First, it may be interesting to government authorities, specifically the CFAs, when designing and sequencing public sector reform strategies, strengthening the budget process, streamlining organizational structures, and improving coordination across central finance functions. Second, the study should assist World Bank teams operating in the countries concerned, by deepening their understanding of the political economy underpinnings of the CFA, and in helping them design, prioritize and sequence their work programs. Third, it may be useful to other stakeholders in the reform process—the legislature, think tanks, academics, donors, and civil society groups—that have an interest in improving the performance and transparency of finance institutions.

The Sector Manager and original Task Team Leader of the stream of work and this report was Jim Brumby. Richard Allen was the Lead Consultant. Other World Bank staff and consultants who made a substantial contribution include Nataliya Biletska, Bjoern Dressel, Verena Fritz, Francesco Grigoli, Nick Howard, Zac Mills, Blanca Moreno-Dodson, Vanya Pasheva, Janet Piller, Emmanuel Pinto Moreira, Adrian Poffley, Fernando Rojas, and Marijn Verhoeven. This report was prepared by Richard Allen, Natalia Biletska, Jim Brumby, Francesco Grigoli, Nick Howard, and Blanca Moreno-Dodson. The authors are especially grateful to Bjoern Dressel for his constructive comments on an earlier draft.

Abbreviations and Acronyms

AFR	Africa Region
BNPP	Bank Netherlands Partnership Program
CAS	country assistance strategy
CFA	Central Finance Agency
CFAA	Country Financial Accountability Assessment
CMU	Country Management Unit
CoG	center of government
CPAR	Country Procurement Assessment Report
CSO	civil society organization
DPM	Deputy Prime Minister
EAP	East Asia and Pacific Region
ECA	Eastern Europe and Central Asia Region
ESW	economic and sector work
FMIS	Financial Management Information System
GDP	gross domestic product
GNI	gross national income
HIPC	heavily indebted poor countries
ICR	Implementation Completion Report
ICT	information and communication technology
IDA	International Development Association
IFI	International Finance Institution
IFMIS	Integrated Financial Management Information System
IMF	International Monetary Fund
KTF	Korean Trust Fund
LAC	Latin America and the Caribbean Region
LIC	low-income country
LICUS	low-income countries under stress
LMIC	low-middle-income country
LTAs	local technical assistants
MNA	Middle East and North Africa Region

MoF	Ministry of Finance
MOFED	Ministry of Finance and Economic Development
MTEF	Medium-Term Expenditure Framework
NIE	New Institutional Economics
NPM	New Public Management
NRA	National Revenue Authority
OECD	Organisation for Economic Co-operation and Development
PEFA	Public Expenditure and Financial Accountability
PER	Public Expenditure Review
PFM	Public Financial Management
PREM	Poverty Reduction and Economic Management
PforR	Performance-for-Results Lending Instrument (World Bank)
ROSC	Reports on Standards and Codes (IMF/World Bank)
SAR	South Asia Region
SOE	state-owned enterprise
SWPs	sector working parties
TOR	Terms of Reference
VAT	value added tax
WBI	World Bank Institute

Executive Summary

This report presents the findings of a study of functions carried out by Central Finance Agencies (CFAs) that was financed jointly by the Bank Netherlands Partnership Program (BNPP), the Korean Trust Fund (KTF) and the World Bank over a three-year period from July 2008 to mid-2011. The work involved the preparation of a framework paper by Bjoern Dressel and Jim Brumby, which employs political economy considerations in its approach to Public Financial Management; a set of case studies involving missions to ten low-income countries, six of which are in the Africa region; and a database on the role and structure of CFAs in 55 countries at various stages of development. In order to test the robustness and versatility of the framework, and based on country background, the missions employed a variety of team structures and approaches.

Chapter 1 of the report defines the concept of a CFA—which is the array of government organizations (including notably the finance ministry) that carry out 16 core finance functions of government (budget preparation and execution, tax policy and revenue administration, procurement, and so on), that are central to the management of public finances. The study gives a strong emphasis to the "political economy" underpinnings of CFAs, including the incentives of and the interrelationships among the main players in public finance, namely the executive branch of government, the legislature, and external players such as IFIs, donors and civil society groups.

Chapter 2 summarizes the main issues and themes arising from the case studies. Substantial progress was made in identifying institutional factors that affect the capabilities of CFAs, including their organizational structures, linkages with stakeholders, availability and use of staff with appropriate skills in economics, accountancy and finance, and efficient use of HR and ICT systems. The chapter presents several examples of how political economy factors affect the incentives and behavior of CFAs in the countries studied, and relates these findings to the various dimensions of the framework paper. Indications from the case studies are that the work was well received by the authorities and is having a positive impact (for example, in Ghana, a new organizational structure of the finance ministry, based on the mission's recommendations, has been adopted).

Chapter 3 describes the CFA database and the questionnaire that was used by Country Management Units (CMUs) and others in compiling it.

The questionnaire contained three parts covering, respectively, the role and responsibilities of the finance ministry and other CFAs; the staffing, skills and gender composition of the CFAs; and the use of ICT systems. The analysis demonstrates the wide mixture of experience that exists across countries. This chapter also presents analytical and country support for an interesting "inverted U-curve" hypothesis, namely that middle-income countries generally have CFA functions more concentrated in the finance ministry than low-income and high-income countries, for different reasons. While the former have more CFA functions unidentified, underdeveloped and performed *de facto* by agencies other than the finance ministry, often being fragmented and inconsistent with its policy goals, the later have more sophisticated levels of distribution and specialization of functions to other CFAs usually in a manner consistent with overall finance ministry goals. In addition, in most countries policy functions are generally more concentrated in the finance ministry than operational functions. Fragile states appear to have CFAs relatively more concentrated than nonfragile ones due to the strong need to perform a few basic public finance functions, while resource-rich countries show generally lower concentration among CFAs; notably those in charge of revenue management tend to be more independent from the finance ministry. These findings are in line with theoretical arguments set out in the report and should stimulate further and deeper research.

Chapter 4 presents the main conclusions and operational implications of the study. "Political economy" analysis is not only important but fundamental to successful strengthening of CFAs. Many proposed initiatives may be viable at a technical level but deemed impracticable from a political economy point of view. Political economy analysis often touches on sensitive issues associated with reform resistance from country authorities, but it can add value to World Bank operations, when combined with relevant technical assessments. Further use of political economy dimensions in PFM analysis may require the development of new skills by the Bank (for example, in political science and change management) but, most importantly, it will require access to the knowledge gained from years of experience in the specific country, allowing a thorough understanding of a country's political dynamics. Finally, the collection of basic data on staff numbers and ICT systems operating in CFAs is also important to understand how CFAs work and such data collection could be standardized across the Bank, if for no other purpose than to allow Bank staff to answer inquiries from clients as to how they compare organizationally with their peers and others.

Chapter 4 also sets out several recommendations on work that could be done by the Bank to follow up on the CFA study and to operationalize the framework. These recommendations include the following:

- Using political economy analysis in PFM before launching new lending operations, in advising on their sequencing and prioritization, and during preparation, implementation, and supervision

- Investing in the development of a continuing dialogue with political leaders and other stakeholders who can be instrumental in driving the PFM reform effort
- Refocusing CFA reform strategies on "best fit" solutions rather than "best practice" models
- Providing more advice to country clients on change management practices and efficient project implementation
- Developing deep country and stakeholder knowledge of political economy aspects of PFM reforms
- Developing procedures to collect basic data on CFAs organizational structures and staffing on a routine basis.

Key messages for finance ministers and other CFA policy makers include the following:

- Promote initiatives that stand a reasonable prospect of success and which are deeply owned by the country, which in part will be influenced by being able to do the following:
- Build partnerships with ministers and groups, such as the legislature, external audit authorities and civil society, who can help push forward the reform effort.
- Be realistic about the reforms that can be achieved within a finite period and about appropriate sequencing.

The report also proposes the outline of a possible performance-related toolkit—perhaps linked to the Bank's new "Program-for-Results" new financing instrument—that could be used to assess and reinforce the capabilities of CFAs, according to the main criteria set out in the Dressel-Brumby framework. The toolkit would help finance ministries improve their capabilities in delivering effective advice on policy issues relating to the budget and public finances, in a similar way that the best performing central banks deliver effective advice on monetary and exchange rate policy.

The report contains two appendixes: the methodology used in preparing the questionnaire; and a one-page summary of each case study report.

CHAPTER 1

Introduction

In July 2008, the World Bank, with financial support from the Bank Netherlands Partnership Program (BNPP), launched a study of *Enhancing the Capabilities of Central Finance Agencies* (CFAs). The task team which carried out the study comprised a group of World Bank staff and consultants;[1] in addition, many other World Bank staff and consultants participated in or contributed to the various case studies. The present report presents the main findings of the study. Further information can be found in the individual case study reports, and the responses to the CFA Questionnaire described below.

What Are CFAs, and Why Are They Important?

CFAs are not a single organization or entity of government but a group of ministries and agencies, of which the ministry of finance (MoF) is normally the most prominent, with collective responsibility for the design and implementation of a country's vast array of financial and fiscal policies and operations. Such policies and operations include macrofiscal analysis and forecasting, budget preparation and execution, accounting and reporting, cash and debt management, fiscal risk analysis, public procurement, tax policy and customs/revenue administration, and the regulation of financial institutions. In this report, the term "CFAs" is used as short hand for ministries and agencies that play a significant role in undertaking such functions. These functions can be divided for convenience into the 16 different categories shown in table 1.1.

In most developing countries, the role of CFAs is the public resources nexus of all issues with a political economy dimension. This is particularly the case in the so-called "limited access order" countries (that is, nondemocratic low-income countries) (see North et al. 2007) where the role and responsibility of the finance ministry largely reflects the consensus of the political and business elite on how to use public resources to help maintain the prevailing political order. In contrast, in "open access order" countries (mainly higher income countries with more advance democratic regimes), the finance ministry's role and responsibilities are largely

Table 1.1 Typical Central Finance Functions

Macroeconomic forecasting, analysis and fiscal policy
Tax policy
Budget preparation and analysis
Public investment management
Aid and debt management
Financial assets and liabilities
Intergovernmental fiscal relations
Treasury and cash management
Accounting and reporting
Internal audit
Public procurement
Civil service pay
Financial sector regulations
Financial framework for managing State-Owned Enterprises (SOEs)
Tax revenues and customs administration
Public Financial Management (PFM) reform coordination

defined by the goal of maximizing public resources for the public good. In reality, as discussed in this report, the category into which a country falls is crucially important in determining what reform path is desirable and politically feasible.[2]

The allocation of roles and responsibilities for central finance functions among the finance ministry itself and other government agencies varies substantially from country to country. There is no "best practice" model,[3] but an effective organization of CFAs is likely to result in improved fiscal outcomes.[4] Some countries have a highly centralized structure, including a finance ministry with very broad powers; other countries have a much more decentralized and fragmented structure (chapter 3 of this reportanalyses the extent of fragmentation across countries and regions). Moreover, the responsibilities of the finance ministry in some advanced countries are typically greater than in many developing countries, where the finance ministry's mandate is often quite restricted. Some finance ministries (for example, those in Germany, the United Kingdom, Japan and Korea) have a wider responsibility for economic strategy and management, making them in effect "super-ministries" of economics and finance.[5] Other countries have preferred to establish a specialized ministry, which can be a reasonable approach when human capacity is weak and both substantial public finance consolidation and restructuring of financial management systems are required.[6] The terminology applied to finance ministries also differs from country to country: for example, some countries use the term "Treasury," others "Ministry of Finance" or "Department of Finance."

Methodological Framework for the Study

As previously indicated, the framework for the present study is set out in Dressel and Brumby (2009). The paper firmly places the functions of a CFA within the wider political economy context of a country. To do so, it first

Figure 1.1 The Political Economy Environment of CFAs

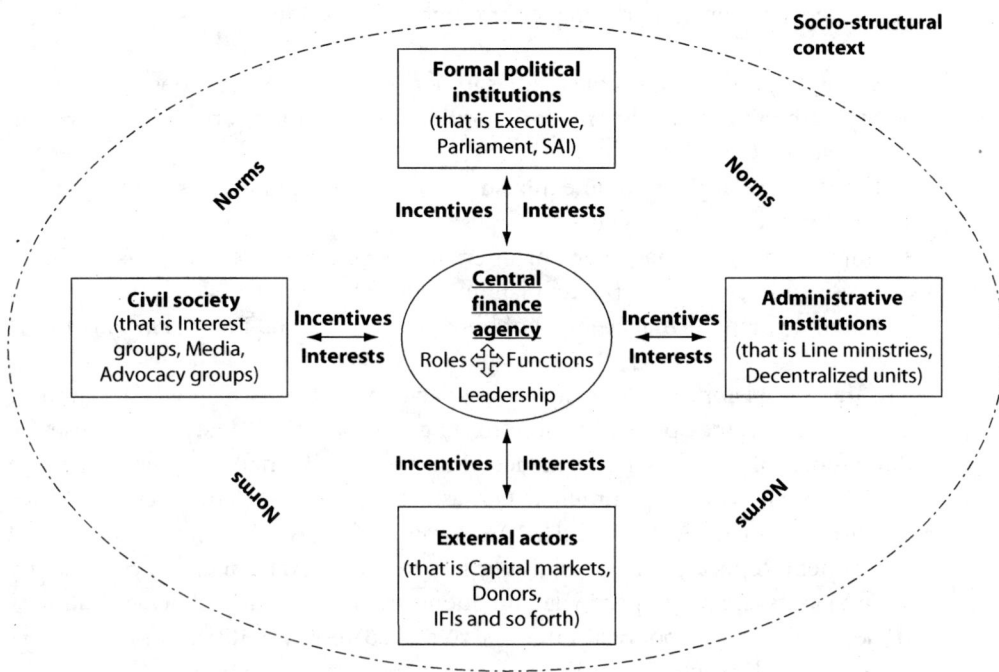

Source: Dressel and Brumby 2009.

draws attention to five critical *institutional* interfaces that shape the activities of the CFA—formal political institutions, administrative institutions, civil society, external actors, and within the CFA itself (figure 1.1). Equally important, it also urges to take account of the socio-structural context in which they are embedded. Structural constraints, such as climate, level of development, degree of ethnic fragmentation and availability of natural resources, constitute boundaries within which political economy dynamics unfold. For example, in some countries, citizens identify so strongly with their place of residence that they define their relationship with the state (their political interests) primarily in terms of their local community. Also, political competition and conflict may be organized mainly around place, ethnicity and language rather than class or ideology; as a consequence, there is often a regular conflict over distribution of resources rather than over ideological frontiers. Hence, the framework offers a comprehensive analytical framework to understand and explore the functioning of the CFA in different country settings (see Dressel and Brumby, 2009, 20-21).

The Dressel-Brumby framework distinguishes importantly between the capacity and capability of CFAs. In practice, many countries have focused attention on building **capacity**, with less emphasis on strengthening the **capability** of CFAs. "Capacity" refers to the volume or scope of inputs such as human resources or ICT systems. "Capability" focuses on how such volumes can be converted into better performance through mechanisms such as:

- Clarifying roles and responsibilities in performing CFA functions
- Strengthening arrangements for coordination and information-sharing within and across CFAs
- Clarifying relations with line ministries, civil society groups, development partners and other stakeholders
- Improving the management of internal business processes such as decision-making hierarchies, corporate planning, and information systems
- Strengthening the management of human resources, and internal incentives.[7]

The traditional approach of increasing capacity may ignore the political economy constraints that may prevent it from turning into capability. The study focuses on dimensions of a CFA's performance that are not normally captured through traditional analytical instruments such as a Public Expenditure Review (PER), Country Financial Accountability Assessment (CFAA), Country Procurement Assessment Reports (CPARs), or Public Expenditure and Financial Accountability (PEFA) assessment—in particular, functional strengths and weaknesses, and how these are related to political interests, roles and responsibilities, and the CFA's organizational structure, staffing and governance arrangements.

The same idea may be expressed as follows: modernizing CFAs requires improving its effectiveness to deliver advice on economic and financial policy and execute functions relevant to these areas across a broad spectrum. The "production function" of a CFA involves several key factors, some of which are often neglected, such as the culture, morale and incentives of the organization; the quality and experience of its management and staff; the organizational structure; the business processes that support and underpin the organization; and the supporting information and human resource management systems. Strengthening relations with the other main actors shown in figure 1.1 is also crucially important. These factors interact with each other, and solutions to one (for example, an improved organizational chart or introduction of a new ICT system) will not necessarily deal with inefficiencies in the other, and are likely to have limited impact if progress is not made along several fronts that deal with other perceived areas of weakness.

In undertaking the case studies, the task team found it useful to draw a distinction between, on the one hand, the **internal** capability of the finance ministry, by which we mean the ability of the ministry (and specifically the minister) to **directly** influence the ministry's effectiveness—for example, by taking actions to reorganize the departments and units of the ministry, improve the use of ICT systems, increase the intake of graduate economists and professional accountants and so on—and, on the other hand, to change the ability to influence those factors **external** to the ministry which, nevertheless, may have a strong impact on the ministry's effectiveness in undertaking public finance functions. Such external influences are largely determined by the ministry's relationships with other key players in the financial management process. In general, while the minister of finance is able to control his ministry's internal capability, he or she will have much less influence over the external factors noted above. This has important implications for the practical implementation of the Dressel-Brumby framework, as we shall discuss below.

An understanding of the structure and interrelationships among CFAs is important because CFAs are responsible for managing a country's public finances and, as a result, exercise a powerful influence on a country's economic and social development. Moreover, conventional instruments for analyzing public financial management (PFM) systems focus primarily on the formal, technical characteristics of these systems and may pay relatively less attention to analyzing the informal rules and incentives which shape the CFAs and affect their operational efficiency, or the relationships among the various players, as explained in the Dressel-Brumby paper. These nontechnical factors are described in this report as "political economy" factors. To assess the capabilities of CFAs, an assessment of these political economy influences on incentives and behavior of key actors is not only desirable but essential.

The recommendations contained in most technical assistance reports prepared by the World Bank, the International Monetary Fund (IMF) and other donor organizations, while thoroughly analyzed and justified at a technical level may not take into account consistently the political economy factors and, consequently, may fall short of assisting policy makers in effectively strengthening CFAs and PFM systems. A failure to address political economy factors may also explain at least in part why some initiatives for reforming PFM systems are not implemented fully, and why *de jure* reforms (that is, changes in the legal framework or other formal rules) tend to be more successful than *de facto* reforms (see Andrews 2010). By analyzing the political economy factors more thoroughly, potential road-blocks and constraints to reform initiatives can be identified, recommendations that are nonrunners politically weeded out and change management programs proposed to facilitate the path of implementing the proposed reforms and ensuring they are sustained.

Political economy analysis can reveal important differences in preferences and incentives across institutions, which may influence the priorities and policy judgments of CFAs, and introduce serious inefficiencies in the quality of management and decision making on public finances. For example, an independent revenue agency may share responsibilities for revenue forecasting with the ministry of finance, and/or with the ministry of planning. The revenue agency, arguably, has an incentive to underproject the future path of government revenues in order to more easily achieve the performance targets set by the finance ministry. The planning ministry on the other hand may have an incentive to overproject revenues, as well as the overall rate of economic growth, in order to demonstrate that the country's poverty-reduction targets are being achieved, thus making the country attractive to foreign investors and the donors who provide overseas development assistance. In this context, the finance ministry may take a neutral position, since its incentive is to present a fiscal position that is stable and consistent with targets and performance benchmarks established in the context of programs agreed with the IMF, the World Bank, and other institutions. Any reform that attempts to harmonize the forecasting function, but fails to take account of the relationships and interactions between these players, is unlikely to be successful.

Another example, frequently found in developing countries, is the separation of the treasury function from other parts of the finance ministry. Some degree of specialization of the accounting and payment functions, perhaps involving separation for control purposes, from other finance operations is necessary, of course, but not if it results in a loss of quality control by the finance minister of the core accounting and reporting operations of government. In some countries, the accountant-general has become an official with a *de facto* rank that is more or less equivalent to the minister to whom he or she is formally responsible, and lines of accountability become blurred or nonexistent.[8] In such cases (the case study of Ghana provides a recent example), the finance minister may be somewhat powerless to institute a functional review of the accountant-general's department, thus preserving an organizational structure that is suboptimal in terms of effective management of public finances. Other examples of how political economy factors may impact on and distort public finance processes are provided in figure 1.1.

Objectives and Outputs of the CFA Study

The main objectives of the study are to assess the following:

- The usefulness and applicability in the field of a political economy approach as outlined by the Dressel-Brumby framework, and whether it should be modified for future applications
- The implications of the study for the future development of diagnostic work on CFAs and public financial management systems, and for the design of the lending and technical assistance operations carried out by the World Bank and other donors

In addition, through the database, the study attempts to analyze:

- To what extent the degree of concentration and fragmentation in central finance functions vary among countries at different stages of development, different administrative traditions and different regions, and what lessons can be drawn.

The main outputs of the study comprise the present report, a set of 10 country reports submitted to the national authorities and related "political economy" notes, and the dataset describing the organization and structure of CFAs in 55 countries.

It is expected that the findings of the study will be of interest to several audiences. First, for the national authorities, specifically the CFAs, in designing and sequencing public sector reform strategies, strengthening the budget process and streamlining organizational structures and improving coordination across central finance functions. Second, the study will assist the World Bank teams operating in the countries concerned, by deepening their understanding of the political economy underpinnings of the CFA, and in helping them design, prioritize and sequence their work programs. Third, it will interest other stakeholders in the reform process—the legislature, think tanks, academics, donors and civil society groups—that have an interest in improving the performance and transparency of finance institutions.

Organization of the Study

The overarching study comprised four main components. First, work on the analytical paper by Dressel and Brumby setting out the basic framework of analysis was completed in July 2009. Second, a series of 10 in-depth country case studies of low-income countries (LICs), mainly in Africa, was carried out between November 2009 and February 2011. Third, a database of CFAs in a cross-section of 55 countries, including low-income, middle-income and high-income countries, was prepared on the basis of a questionnaire described in chapter 3. These sources of information were supplemented, where required, by a range of other documents and technical assistance reports prepared by staff of the World Bank and the IMF.

In order to select countries for the case studies, and agree upon suitable terms of reference, the task team entered into discussions with country teams from the various regional departments of the World Bank, which in turn sought the approval of the country authorities—in most cases the finance minister. This process occupied much of the task team's time during the first nine months of 2010. In addition, a few missions were cancelled or postponed, often for internal political reasons, such as elections or cabinet reshuffling. As a result, completion of the field work was delayed into the first quarter of 2011, and as noted a six-month extension of the BNPP grant was requested and approved.

The task team attempted to select a group of countries that incorporate diverse characteristics in relation to criteria such as the size of population, the presence or absence of significant mineral resources, an Anglophone or Francophone administrative culture, and a presidential or parliamentary system of government, so that the implications of these variables can be analyzed. The countries that agreed, after discussion with the CMUs and the country authorities, to participate in the case studies include six countries from Africa (Benin, Cameroon, Chad, Ghana, Rwanda and Sierra Leone), two countries from East Asia and the Pacific (Mongolia and Tonga), one country from the Middle East and North Africa (the Republic of Yemen) and one country from Latin America and the Caribbean (Nicaragua). As required by the terms of the BNPP grant, all the countries concerned are classified as low income.[9] However, the inclusion of higher income countries in the statistical database provides benchmarks against which the CFAs in the 10 countries included in the sample can be compared.

To test the versatility and robustness of the Dressel-Brumby framework, the case studies—most of which comprised a two-week mission to the country concerned by a team of staff and experts[10]—experimented with a variety of topics, approaches and modalities. The mission teams comprised a varying mix of staff, international consultants and local consultants. As discussed further in chapter 2, the scope of the CFA mission was largely determined by the interests and requirements of the CMU and the government, and the task team was required to reconcile the requests of the country authorities and the objectives of the study itself. In some of the case studies (for example, Cameroon and Tonga), the mission team analyzed finance functions across a relatively broad spectrum; in other cases, as described in chapter 2, the team focused on a narrower range of topics, determined through discussion with the CMU and country authorities. At the end of each mission, the mission team presented the authorities (usually the Minister of Finance) with a draft report of its findings and recommendations. The report was subsequently revised in light of comments received from the authorities and peer reviewers in the World Bank, before being formally submitted to the authorities by the Bank's country management unit (CMU).

Structure of the Report

The remainder of the report comprises the following chapters:

- Chapter 2 evaluates the lessons learned from conducting the case studies, and presents important issues and themes that emerged from this fieldwork.
- Chapter 3 sets out the findings of the CFA database in relation to the organization of central finance functions in the 55 countries covered, and issues concerning the staffing levels of CFAs, their gender balance and use of information technology (ICT).
- Chapter 4 discusses the implications of the study for the future work of the World Bank and other development partners. It also presents in outline a proposal for a new performance-related assessment tool, based on the Dressel-Brumby framework that will help ministries of finance strengthen their capabilities and become centers of excellence in public finance.
- Finally, the report includes two appendixes that provide further information on the case studies; a description of the questionnaire and methodology used in preparing the database (appendix A); and a one-page summary of the ten case studies (appendix B), the full reports of which are available on demand.[11]

Notes

1. The Sector Manager and original Task Team Leader of the report was Jim Brumby. Richard Allen was the Lead Consultant. Other World Bank staff and consultants who made a substantial contribution include Nataliya Biletska, Bjoern Dressel, Verena Fritz, Francesco Grigoli, Nick Howard, Zac Mills, Vanya Pasheva, Janet Piller, Emmanuel Pinto Moreira, Adrian Poffley, and Fernando Rojas. The synthesis report was prepared by Richard Allen, Francesco Grigoli, Nick Howard and Blanca Moreno-Dodson. The authors are especially grateful to Bjoern Dressel for his constructive comments on an earlier draft.

2. The example of Uganda is very instructive in this regard. In the early days of the Museveni regime, in the mid-1990s, the need to gain legitimacy and to deliver quick gains to the people enabled the finance ministry to enact and implement progressive PFM reform. The finance minister was given the political space to take the necessary initiatives. More recently, the political leadership's energy has been geared towards political survival, and the space to implement further PFM reforms is very limited. Some reforms made in the 1990s, for example, the medium-term expenditure framework (MTEF), have regressed.

3. For a discussion of comparative CFA structures in a range of advanced countries, with special reference to France, Germany and the United Kingdom, see Allen and Kohnert (2012).

4. Here we refer to three types of fiscal outcomes: fiscal discipline, allocative efficiency and technical efficiency.

5. France was another example until 2008 when the ministry was divided into separate ministries of economy and public finance.

6. The size of the finance ministry can vary widely, from around 100 staff or even fewer in some small countries to many thousands of staff in others, depending on the range of activities carried out and the efficiency of the organization.

7. The two concepts are linked: where capacity is low, capabilities are also likely to be constrained. A weak configuration and/or organization of inputs, and a high-cost operating environment, perhaps marked by a lack of authority, may mean that even when capacity is high, capability may be low. See Dressel and Brumby (2009, 2–3). Note that Organisation for Economic Co-operation and Development (OECD) and World Bank Institute (WBI) definitions of capacity are closer to our definition of capability.

8. Similarly, in one middle-eastern country, a recent director-general of the budget, while nominally part of the finance ministry, claimed for himself and his staff independent authority under a separate act of law which established the budget office. In this claim he was supported by the patronage of the royal family. Consequently, the finance minister was unable to consolidate the operations of his ministry under one roof.

9. Specifically, countries with a gross national income (GNI) below US$1,135 per capita, and are eligible to borrow from the International Development Association (IDA).

10. An exception was the mission to Tonga which was of one week's duration, was combined with a mission to Tonga by the Australian Department of Finance and comprised a single expert.

11. From the World Bank's Public Sector Governance external website.

CHAPTER 2

Analysis of the Case Studies

In this chapter, we summarize the findings of the 10 case studies, and address issues that include the following:

- How useful is the Dressel-Brumby framework as an operational tool to be applied in the field?
- How has this framework, which employs political economy considerations, helped further the understanding of Central Finance Agencies (CFAs) and Public Financial Management (PFM) processes in developing countries?
- What are the main lessons emerging from the case studies that can be applied in further work?

While the CFA study was not intended to test broader political science theories about the relationship between institutions and public finance processes, the case study findings nevertheless provide interesting insights into the functioning of various political regimes (for example, presidential, neo-patrimonial and hybrid systems) precisely because a wider political economy lens was applied and new empirical evidence was unearthed.

Design of the Case Studies

As discussed in chapter 1, an analysis of "political economy" factors is a crucial element in understanding how CFAs and PFM systems function, and the main levers that drive decision making on the budget and other areas of fiscal policy. Political economy analysis is important to ensure that initiatives to strengthen CFAs and PFM systems, as well as being technically sound, are politically acceptable and compatible with the incentives of the national authorities and donors, so that their implementation does not experience the constraints and resistance to change that are often found in low-income countries (LICs). Such factors are also important to consider at the individual-agent level: successful reforms are dependent on the internalization of both the problem and the solution, and political economy analysis has the potential to assist with better understanding the motivation and incentives necessary to achieve development

objectives. This is true not only in the field of CFAs and public finance, but in
other activities and projects supported by the Bank which require the direct
involvement or intermediation of government institutions (in practice, this
means all operations).

As noted in chapter 1, conventional diagnostic instruments such as the Public
Expenditure and Financial Accountability (PEFA) assessment tool, Public
Expenditure Reviews (PERs) and Country Financial Accountability Assessments
(CFAAs), and the International Monetary Fund's (IMF's) Fiscal Transparency
studies, focus mainly on technical issues, such as whether budgets get approved
on time, what systems of internal control and internal audit are applied, whether
the procurement system meets international standards of acceptability, whether
there exists a genuinely independent external audit body, what are the rules and
procedures for making budget documents available to the public and so on.
While such instruments may pay relatively little direct attention to political
economy factors—such as the relationship between formal and informal rules of
behavior, the incentives of bureaucrats and politicians to act in accordance with
formal rules, the relationship between the various governmental agencies and
civil society groups comprising the CFA, and the strength of the political leadership that is required to carry reform initiatives through to implementation—
they provide a useful platform for political economy "drilling."

It became apparent to the CFA task team in carrying out the present study
that there are significantly greater practical difficulties in applying a framework
that encompasses "political economy" factors than a conventional diagnostic
analysis of PFM issues, such as a PEFA assessment. The difficulties experienced
by the task teams include resistance to openly discussing with donors or third
parties: issues of relationships with other individuals, departments and agencies,
especially where such relationships are politically sensitive or problematic; areas
of the PFM system issues that are significantly affected by rent seeking and perhaps corrupt practices; central finance functions where ownership and quality
of outcomes are not in general agreement; and issues that are seen as the pre-
rogative of the minister, and on which more junior officials are often reluctant
to express a personal opinion.

In designing each mission, it also became clear to the task team that political
economy is a sensitive topic between Bank staff and country authorities. The
nature of political economy analysis requires putting issues in the open that
have often not been openly talked about. Such dialogue, while critically important to the design of good policies and reform initiatives, may have an adverse
impact on other areas of engagement.[1] As a result, in some cases, the task team
was either discouraged from conducting the CFA study, or faced pressure to
steer the terms of reference for the study into the more technical areas—such
as an evaluation of the functions carried out by the CFA and its organizational
structure—that avoid discussion of sensitive issues. For reasons discussed further
in chapter 4, in some countries, this issue of sensitivity is likely to constitute an
obstacle to extending the case study approach into a more general application

of political economy analysis in Bank diagnostic studies, or to be mainstreamed in the PEFA assessment framework. Nevertheless, the task team takes the view that political economy analysis has an important role to play in countries where the authorities have a strong incentive—and the leadership required—to improve existing institutions. In chapter 4, we present the outline of a tool that could be developed for that purpose, drawing on elements of the Dressel-Brumby framework, and the findings of the present study.

As a consequence of these pressures and constraints, the mission teams had to make some adjustments to the scope of the CFA study in order to comply with the requirements and priorities of the national authorities. Examples include analyzing the scope for strengthening the internal capabilities of the central finance ministry (Chad, Ghana, Rwanda, the Republic of Yemen); reviewing the relationship between the ministry of finance and the ministry of economy and planning (Mongolia, Benin, and the Republic of Yemen); strengthening the public investment management system (Cameroon, Mongolia, Nicaragua); and clarifying the role and relationships of the finance ministry, central bank and ministry of economy and planning in undertaking macroeconomic forecasting and analysis (the Republic of Yemen).

The case studies confirm that the Dressel-Brumby paper provides a useful framework for analyzing the political economy environment within which CFAs operate. However, the framework could usefully be supplemented by additional analysis that "drills down" into concrete issues concerning the capabilities of CFAs and efficiency of PFM processes. Similarly, the technical analysis of PFM systems provided by PEFA assessments, and so on.—which focus on the efficiency of specific areas of financial management need to be supplemented by an assessment of political and institutional conditions if questions such as "are the conditions right to make a reform" and "what kind of reform is needed" are to be answered satisfactory. As discussed in chapter 4, this in turn requires a political economy analysis that is tailored to the precise issues and problems being studied, as argued in Fritz, Kaiser, and Levy (2009). Table 2.1 gives some examples of (hypothetical but not unreal) situations where political economy analysis could deepen the understanding provided by a purely technical evaluation. In effect, such analysis becomes a filter to select initiatives that are compatible with the incentives of politicians and bureaucrats. It may also be possible for the Bank to propose ways in which incentive structures might be strengthened, at the margin, to improve the practicality of certain initiatives and interventions.

Lessons of the Case Studies

The case studies demonstrate that an analysis of political economy factors, when combined with a technical assessment of CFAs, may have considerable value in deepening our understanding of the structure and behavior of CFAs. Indeed, we would argue that such an analysis should be regarded as an essential component

Table 2.1 The Potential Contribution of Political Economy Analysis

Example	Technical analysis	Political economy analysis	Likely Bank response
The prime minister proposes to establish an integrated and centralized National Revenue Authority (NRA). The government asks the Bank to finance the development of the new institution.	The establishment of an integrated revenue authority is in line with guidelines promulgated by, among others, the Bank and the IMF. The current system separates VAT, income tax and customs collections, and efficiency gains are highly likely with the right institutional structures.	The prime minister may be likely to appoint his confidante as head of the NRA. The finance minister, supported by the president of the central bank, strongly opposes the proposal on the basis that tax revenues may be threatened, fiscal policy could destabilize and the influence of the finance ministry on tax policy will be reduced.	The fiscal risks of supporting the proposal are substantial. Out of concern that the decisions are firm to appoint the new head, the Bank may inform the government that it will not support the proposal unless conditions are included to ensure a merit-based structure for appointing the top management, tighten the draft law to strengthen the finance minister's supervisory role and provide an avenue for civil society to monitor performance.
The finance minister makes a proposal to establish a macroeconomic policy and forecasting unit in his ministry, and asks the Bank for technical assistance.	The Bank and IMF examine the quality and consistency of prior macroeconomic forecasts. While the data and reporting have been consistent, major flaws are identified that lead to substantial revisions in projections of GDP and fiscal aggregates.	The proposal is strongly opposed by the minister of economic development, who is also the deputy prime minister (DPM), on the grounds that his ministry already contains a full-fledged macroeconomic unit. The finance minister is similarly a high-placed member of the ruling party and would likely wield substantial influence in preparing the forecasts.	The Bank identifies key technical challenges and primarily recommends that new forecasting models are developed. The finance minister's proposal is politically driven, designed to boost his authority vis-à-vis the DPM is highly political. The Bank may recommend an intermediate solution where forecasting responsibilities remain the same but interministry coordination is improved.
An association of civil society organizations stage demonstrations in the state capital in protest over poor public services and lack of a voice in decisions on the budget and public finances. They ask for the Bank's help in supporting their case.	The Bank analysis reveals that there is a budget process that solicits comments from stakeholders via sector working groups but in practice the budget rarely deviates from the government's initial proposal by more than two percent.	The president and the finance minister are strongly opposed to any increase in the "democratization" of the budget process. Civil society already plays an important role in certain areas, for example, representation on the anticorruption commission.	The Bank needs to be careful not to jeopardize its relationship with the authorities. The Bank may decide to work within the existing sector working group process, initiating a low-key dialogue on how to strengthen and formalize the involvement of civil society in the budget.

Note: NRA = National Revenue Authority; IMF = International Monetary Fund; VAT = value added tax; GDP = gross domestic product; DPM = deputy prime minister, Bank = World Bank.

Table 2.2 Mapping of Main Themes to Dimensions of Dressel-Brumby Framework

	Theme 1	Theme 2	Theme 3	Theme 4
Internal aspects of CFAs	x	x	x	x
Formal political organizations	x	x		
Administrative institutions	x	x		
Civil society				
External actors (for example, donors)				x

of any such diagnosis and if it cannot be carried out, for political or practical reasons, it is likely that the design of strategies to reform CFAs will be flawed and likely to fail. These implications will be discussed further in chapter 4. In the remainder of the present chapter, we provide some main themes, drawn from the case studies of instances where a political economy analysis provides insights that are helpful in enriching our understanding of CFAs and PFM reform strategies (see table 2.2).

The main themes that emerged quite strongly from the case studies:

- The use (or misuse) of presidential power in the budget process
- The practice of fragmenting finance functions among several ministries or agencies in order to dilute the authority of the finance minister; the tendency in LICs for a hierarchy of decision making within the CFA to exist that is much more extreme and rigid than in developed countries
- Uneven success in coordinating the interests and programs of the authorities and those of the donors.

Finally, some of the case studies used political economy analysis in order to filter out potentially weak reform initiatives, and isolate those that are likely to be politically (as well as technically) feasible. For example, the study of Nicaragua discarded eight potential reform initiatives to strengthen public investment management that "do not appear to be feasible in Nicaragua's current political and institutional environment." Some of these initiatives had been successful in other Latin American countries but were not deemed appropriate in the Nicaraguan context. Indications from other case studies are that the work was well received by the authorities and is having a positive impact (in Ghana, for example, the finance ministry has introduced a new organizational structure, based on the mission's recommendations).

Main Theme 1: The Use (and Misuse) of Presidential Power

In several of the countries studied, the head of state plays an important role in making executive decisions on the budget and public finance policy. While such powers are normally exercised within the framework of the constitution and budget law, they are not always compatible with the idea of an efficient and transparent budget process, as described in the literature on public finance. For example, the CFA study on Cameroon interestingly observes that:

> The president has significant influence and discretion with regards to budget planning as well as budget execution. For budget planning, the President issues the budget circular to line ministries. This requirement, moreover, is a source of delay as the circular is only issued in September (in 2010) or even October (in 2009). The president is also the final arbiter for contestations about budget allocations.

And the same report notes that:

> A key marker of governance in Cameroon is inertia. Jeune Afrique recently characterized Cameroon as a "sleeping lion." Inertia is rooted in the combination of a long rule that has entered a sunset period, a hierarchical system which requires top level (i.e., ministerial, PM, or presidential) approval for many decisions even of a rather routine or minor nature, an apparent relative satisfaction with the status quo among elites, and reluctance by those disadvantaged by the status quo to enter into open opposition... The direct role that the head of state plays in many decisions—such as organizational structures, signing off on instructions, etc.—makes change management within ministries and across government challenging.

Similarly, the case study of Benin observes that:

> Executive largesse is a critical factor in decentralized fiscal appropriations; what is little more than administrative clientelism has emerged as a rule in Benin. These actions include the distribution of material benefits, employment opportunities, and access to favors that the executive branch controls. In an environment of chronic fiscal shortages, the importance of administrative clientelism is evident in the use of influence and favoritism the president extends.

Administrative clientelism in Benin is extenuated by the lack of respect for judicial regulations and procedures—formal rules are not binding.

An important implication of this analysis is that large tracts of the fiscal process (for example, any attempt to usurp or weaken the President's discretionary powers in budgeting) are likely to be outside the direct influence of the finance minister, and off limits from a reform perspective.

Main Theme 2: Fragmenting CFAs for Political Gain

As explained in chapter 3, in upper-middle-income and advanced countries it is quite frequent to find CFA functions that are being performed outside the finance ministry, which diminishes concentration in one central agency and offers potential government effectiveness benefits.[2] This process is usually driven both by managerial reasons—for example, the establishment of quasi-autonomous government agencies—as well as technical and technological factors, such as computerization of treasury systems.

On the contrary, most low-income countries have not reached the stage of development where this kind of functional delegation can be undertaken without loss of fiscal control. In those country settings, a different kind of phenomenon has been observed in which public finance functions appear fragmented into different CFAs. Such a structure could be due, for example, to specific actions taken by the head of state to divide the financial power attributed to the minister of finance among several ministers in order to avoid the accumulation of excessive authority in the hands of one person, and to preserve the discretionary powers of the president over spending and revenue collection. Other reasons could simply be found in institutional weaknesses, lack of coordination between the finance ministries and the other CFAs, or even rent-seeking behaviours and political preferences. Although such phenomena are not unknown in advanced countries,[3] there seem to be quite commonplace in low-income countries with weaker institutional capacities. In the Republic of Yemen, for example, the mission team was unable to obtain a clear answer to the question of which minister is responsible for fiscal policy—in practice, this role seems to be divided on a more or less ad hoc basis between the finance minister, the minister of planning and the governor of the central bank. Responsibility for macroeconomic forecasting in the Republic of Yemen is also divided between several different entities, with resulting inefficiencies and uncertainties described in the case study. The result is that fragmentation impedes efficient coordination among government agencies.

Another example is given in the Cameroon report: in 2002, the authorities complied with a condition of the Bank and IMF, as part of the enhanced Heavily Indebted Poor Countries (HIPC) initiative, to merge the ministries of finance and planning but, as soon as the completion point was reached, the ministries were split again.

A further example of the possible fragmentation of finance functions in low-income countries is provided by the case study of Tonga:

> Creation in 2009 of a separate Ministry of Revenue and Customs incorporating the staff from the [finance ministry's] Revenue Services Department, which ended the reporting relationship to the Minister of Finance, has further eroded the tax policy capacity of [the finance ministry] and led to uncertainties about its future responsibilities for certain areas of tax policy.

The case of Mongolia is also relevant here. The parliament plays a dominant role in policy making, and exerts a strong influence on the machinery of government, so as to prevent any one agency from becoming too powerful. As part of its strategy to limit the authority of the finance ministry, the parliament has worked to ensure that finance functions of government are divided among several agencies. The macroeconomic forecasting function was transferred from the finance ministry to a new agency for national economic development, and the two entities were involved in a debate about the allocation of responsibilities for crucially important policy areas such as the public investment program, the budget for capital investment, and the management of public private partner-ships. The parliament has also supported the establishment of a national invest-ment bank which, unless adequate supervision and control arrangements are established, may also undermine the authority of the finance ministry. A suc-cessful resolution of this debate about the allocation of responsibilities for finance and development planning is of critical importance in Mongolia because of the need to exploit, in the next 5–10 years, vast deposits of coal, copper and other mineral resources.

It should be noted that in some low-income countries, the reverse phenom-enon can also be observed: the president has chosen to use the finance minister as an ally in building the economic and financial power of the state, and has given him/her strong powers to do so. Such an alliance also gives a strong momentum to the PFM reform process. It can be observed in Uganda during the 1990s and in Rwanda at the present time. The success of such an approach depends, however, on several factors including the trust of the president for the finance minister, and a common view of economic priorities and the importance of firm fiscal policies. It might be particularly important at the beginning of a regime, when resources are contested and legitimacy is at stake. It can also be observed in some fragile states. The approach may not be sustainable when the views of the president and finance minister on fiscal policies diverge, and initia-tives to strengthen CFAs start to erode.

Main Theme 3: Strengthening the Internal Capability of CFAs

As noted in chapter 1, it was generally easier for the mission teams to make progress in areas in which the internal capability of the CFA was being assessed, namely issues of organizational structure, human resource capability, and so on, which are directly under the control of the CFA officials, and are less influenced or diluted by the minister's relationship with other players such as the office of the president and/or prime minister, line ministries and civil society groups.

The task team developed a methodological framework for analyzing and measuring the internal capability of a CFA which was broken down into the following six dimensions: (a) *organizational structure*, in which the current staffing complement is profiled by sector, educational qualifications and gen-der; (b) *attraction and retention of staff*, which considers the track record of the CFAs in attracting and retaining staff; (c) *performance management*, which assesses the extent to which the CFAs are effectively managing staff perfor-mance; (d) *decentralized decision making*, which discusses where decision-making authority is vested among officials below the minister/vice minister level; (e) *change management*, which looks at the role of leaders of the CFAs in implementing the intended PFM reform agenda, and (f) *information technology*, which gives an overview of the degree to which progress has been made in the implementation of computerized information systems, including the use of email within government agencies.[4] An approach based on this methodology was applied (with some variations) in the case studies of Chad, Ghana, Rwanda and the Republic of Yemen. It proved quite useful, and could readily be applied in other countries, in conjunction with a review of CFA functions and business processes. Examples of issues of interest that emerged from these studies are listed below.

Inadequate staff records. In some of the countries reviewed by the case studies, records on staffing and personnel matters were of generally poor quality. These weaknesses included lack of comprehensive records of the number of staff and consultants employed, and on the academic qualifications of the staff, or their education and training history. The mission teams had to piece together such information from a variety of sources. Nor were there any systematic arrangements for evaluating the performance of employees (see below). In general, central banks were further ahead in maintaining such records, as well as human resource management policies more generally.

Poor systems for recruiting and retaining staff. In many of the countries studied, employment with the CFAs offers high levels of job security coupled with high tolerance of low productivity. With modest demands made of them, most civil servants take secondary employment outside the government to supplement their relatively low compensation. The appointment of consultants—often paid at much higher rates than regular civil servants—to fill line management positions is another familiar practice in many low-income countries (see Main Theme 4 below). Lack of career planning and poor learning opportunities for staff are frequently observed. Some of the case studies highlight how lack of openness in appointing civil servants to key positions in the CFAs seriously undermines the efficiency of recruitment procedures. Such practices include the manipulation of public service examinations for political purposes (Cameroon). And the report on Sierra Leone notes that:

> Generally, while authority in the country may be derived from occupancy of bureaucratic positions, ability to project this authority, particularly in a few ministries like [finance], is often contingent upon concessions and ties to ruling parties. This creates dilemmas for bureaucrats and technocrats: while they derive authority from their political networks in order to be effective as reformers, their success is inevitably associated with their political ties instead of with the merits of their technical or administrative abilities.

Ineffective performance management. In general, CFAs in the countries reviewed do not currently set high performance standards or have effective management processes by which performance of individual employees and the institutions as a whole are assessed, reported, and addressed. There appears to be considerable scope, therefore, to develop basic elements of a performance-related management system: for example, by providing each employee with a job description; setting goals and planning work; measuring progress towards goals and providing feedback; setting high standards of employees whilst developing the skills needed to reach those standards; and using formal and informal rewards to recognize the behaviors and results that accomplish the goals. In several countries, mission teams noted that incentives are not currently oriented towards encouraging or rewarding high performance. In the Republic of Yemen, for example, participation in routine committee meetings warrants the payment of bonuses which constitute a significant proportion of total remuneration.

In several countries, staffing levels in CFAs are unnecessarily high. A consistent theme emerging from the mission's interviews with senior officials (at director-general or director level) was that they are reliant on a small subset of their employees to deliver the sector's work program. Major efficiency improvements are possible by streamlining and/or automating the current business processes and, if this were done, a significantly smaller workforce would be needed. However, such a policy would be politically very sensitive and might be ruled out in many countries.

Inefficient top management structures, and overhierarchical decision-making processes. In many of the countries reviewed, ministers and senior levels of management spend much of their time reviewing, and being expected to take decisions on, detailed matters which, in advanced countries, would be delegated to more junior levels. For example, the case study report of Ghana commented that:

> The role and responsibilities of top management in [the Ministry of Finance and Economic Policy] are characterized by a lack of a clear separation between the political levels of the Ministry and the regular civil service cadre. Most decisions, whether on policy or administrative issues, are ultimately taken by senior management. The Deputies frequently become involved in technical work (e.g., analysis of fiscal trends, or meetings with the Bank of Ghana on fiscal and monetary developments) that in finance ministries with higher capacity and a stronger separation of roles and responsibilities would be routinely carried out by regular civil servants.

Many developed countries by contrast have established arrangements to filter the information that is relayed to the minister of finance for decision, so that he/she can focus on issues of key strategic and policy importance. Two such systems are widely used. In presidential regimes such as France, the cabinet system incorporates a large private office for the minister of high-caliber officials on whom the minister relies for policy advice, and who can deal with day-to-day decisions on minor matters, and request information and analysis from the sectors and departments below.

On the other hand, in parliamentary regimes, such as the Westminster system found in the United Kingdom and many British Commonwealth countries, the Secretary-General (sometimes called the Permanent Secretary or Chief Director) system requires the appointment of a very senior official, at deputy minister or director general level, who is responsible for organizing the work of the ministry on a day-to-day basis, and for channeling documents and issues to the minister which need his personal attention. In many developing countries, the legal and regulatory frameworks, as well as the formal institutional arrangements, do not exist or are unclear regarding how such decisions by the minister of finance are made. To fill this vacuum, senior managers are required *de facto* to retain control over decision making, thus reinforcing a hierarchical culture, and preventing a sensible allocation of responsibility to more junior officials.

Ineffective use of ICT systems. Improving the capability of employees is furthered by the judicious implementation of appropriate technology by which business processes can be automated and employee productivity and efficiency significantly enhanced. Such changes require a climate of openness and transparency in the exchange of ideas and information within the CFA, which needs much further development in many low-income countries. In several of the countries reviewed, the progress made in recent years by the CFAs in introducing technology-based solutions (except in accounting and financial reporting through Financial Management Information System [FMIS] applications) has been modest.

Dener, Watkins, and Dorotinsky (2011) provide an extensive study of FMIS systems that analyzes the technical and political economy factors that can hold back these developments. FMIS projects in which the preconditions for PFM reforms were assessed properly (including the political economy analysis of related information and communication technology [ICT] investments) and a time-bound action plan was developed with realistic sequencing of reform activities tend to produce more effective solutions in relatively shorter time. The continuity of the initial commitment of leaders is crucial to ensure the introduction of necessary changes in business processes and behaviors/mindsets within a reasonable period of time. Success also depends on adequate preparation before the approval of the project (realistic functional and technical requirements, cost/time estimates and procurement/disbursement plans). Lack of attention to change management (see below), and to building consensus among the players (including most importantly the line ministries that must use the systems) is one of the main reasons for delay and (in some cases) failure. In Ghana, for example, an Integrated Financial Management Information System (IFMIS) launched in 2001 is still technically in its pilot phase, and has been replaced by a new US$40 million initiative supported by the Bank and donors.

In addition, few of the low-income countries studied (except Rwanda) used email in a comprehensive and efficient way (though the majority of middle-income countries do—captured in the survey reported wider usage of email and ICT systems). In some countries, for example Ghana and the Republic of Yemen, officials in the finance ministry were allocated official email accounts but these were rarely used because of problems of connectivity, lack of consistent access to computers that are necessary to check such accounts or fears that information might be leaked or misused by other colleagues (especially in the absence of necessary ICT control and oversight mechanisms). In such countries officials generally prefer to use their private email accounts. The result is not only inefficiency in business processes, but loss of essential institutional knowledge.[5]

Main Theme 4: Strengthening Coordination of CFA Reforms

The case studies provide support for an important phenomenon that has been noted in the literature, namely that weak coordination among donors—and between donors and their clients in finance and planning ministries—can pose a problem in designing and implementing coherent strategies for reforming CFAs and PFM systems. Incentives affecting donors and finance ministries are not always mutually consistent. Additionally, in some countries, it is not easy to identify a guiding coalition of leaders who have the political authority to implement change and who are ready to act collectively over a sustained time period in order to bring about the necessary reform objectives.

While for many donors formal review processes during loan preparation provide input to the technical design and the vast volume of procedural requirements, they do not always provide input and checks on the political economy aspects of the loans. Several issues emerge.

First, there might be a tendency for donors to bundle together a large number of lending initiatives which are beyond the government's capacity to implement them; second, there is typically a related tendency for donors to be too optimistic about the time period it will take to implement the reforms. The use of "basket funding," in which donors pool their resources into a single fund, and slice up the reform program into pieces for which each of them take responsibility, has advantages in terms of alignment behind a common agenda, use of one lending modality rather than several, and reducing the transactions costs for clients. At the same time, it may exacerbate the risk for reform programs to grow beyond the capability of either the donors or the client to implement effectively.

On the other hand, governments in low-income countries may actively encourage the Bank and other donors to provide large loans as they contribute to increasing their status regionally and internationally, and may even provide a source of economic rents.

Reforms of CFAs and PFM in many lower-income countries are not always sufficiently demand driven. Studies, including the latest PEFA evaluation by Lawson and Folscher (2011), confirm that the ownership of PFM reforms by client governments is often weak, especially in low-income countries. Moreover, governments may have relatively little experience of the technical aspects of PFM reforms, and rely heavily on the advice of experts from advanced countries. Such experts may recommend finance ministers to proceed with reforms that are insufficiently related to local needs and capabilities, as described in Allen (2008). As countries move into middle-income status, this pattern tends to change as the capabilities of finance ministries and their exposure to new ideas and technological possibilities increase, and they learn to interact with donors more efficiently.

There may be an understated mutual complicity between donors and CFAs. On PFM, it may be that donors understand their inability to see significant reforms move forward. And yet they do not wish to declare failure and walk away (they need to lend, have programs, keep staff occupied, and so on). And senior CFA officials fully understand this. This may lead to reforms being agreed upon on the form without substantial changes occurring in the function.

A related issue is that countries may not have the human capacity to implement the reforms that they agree to implement with the support of the donor community. As a result, it is commonly observed that CFAs supplement their regular staff positions with consultants and advisors financed by the donors, which does not always contribute to building and reinforcing ownership. This may become a particular problem in fragile states. Such advisors often take responsibility for line management positions and, once hired, are difficult to move out. More important, they may permanently weaken the capability of the CFAs to build local capability to fill the positions concerned. For example, the CFA study for Sierra Leone notes that:

> "Local Technical Assistants" (LTAs) are on contracts that can be terminated by either party on one month's notice, and are paid as much as 10 times their civil service counterparts. The LTAs were recruited into units within the Ministry of Finance and Economic Development (MOFED) by donors such as DFID, the EC, the AfDB, and the World Bank starting in 2002. They were originally intended to be a short term resource to substitute for a lack of capacity to implement needed reforms. However, they have since taken on core line functions in MOFED, and are considered to provide the main technical capability within the Ministry. Their enhanced conditions appear to have become attached to the individuals concerned, not to the positions they hold. With the partial exception of staff of the Accountant General and Administration Departments, most finance units are staffed by LTAs. Overall, they accounted for 40percent of the workforce as at October 2008, and 85 percent of the wage bill.

The aid effectiveness agenda (on the efficient management and use of overseas development assistance) has seen, donors and their client governments agreeing to make greater use of national systems of budgeting, treasury, procurement, audit and so on. While such agreement has been viewed by some commentators as an incentive that promotes the development of improved national systems and stronger CFAs, it also raises difficult issues about the readiness of countries to take on these additional responsibilities without increasing fiduciary risk, a result which would be the reverse of the stated objective of the policy.

Notes

1. Some Country Management Units (CMUs) argued that they already had a sufficient understanding off the "political economy" issues that surround the management of public finances. However, to augment this, the task team recommends that CMUs consider undertaking a more concerted effort to capture political economy analysis (see chapter 4 for specific suggestions) and to consider ways to make better use of the results in their policy dialogues.

2. The literature suggests there could be some beneficial microeconomic effects due to the specialization of the new agencies.

3. For example, countries such as Australia, Brazil, Canada, France, Korea, and the United States all have divided finance ministries. In most of these countries, political factors—notably an attempt to dilute the authority of the finance minister—played an important role in the decision to split these functions. See Allen and Kohnert (2012).

4. A similar framework is proposed in Dressel and Brumby (2009), table 4.

5. Besides looking at websites and email usage, this study did not undertake a complete assessment of the current status of ICT system in CFAs based on a well-established control framework to clarify important aspects of PFM information systems, identify gaps, and define a roadmap for possible improvements.

CHAPTER 3

The Database—Analysis of the Organization of the CFA Functions

In this chapter, we set out an analysis of the cross-country data that were compiled by the Central Finance Agency (CFA) task team. The database was prepared using a questionnaire that was sent to World Bank country teams, country economists and public sector specialists in a range of countries. Appendix A contains the questionnaire and describes the methodology in detail. Overall the responses to the questionnaire were only partially satisfactory.[1] On the whole, the database provides valuable information on the organization and staffing of CFAs that was not previously available from other sources. However, it would be useful in future research to extend the number of countries covered, and the range of questions asked, so that the analysis of the results can be deepened. In addition, the Bank should invest more resources in collecting systematically, basic data on CFAs, including the staff numbers employed in various functions, entities and categories, gender breakdown and the use of information and communication technology (ICT) systems and email.

Based on the database, the analysis focuses on the extent to which CFA functions and activities are concentrated in the hands of one agency—usually the Ministry of Finance (MoF)—and to what extent they are distributed among other agencies of government. For this purpose, two measures of concentration were used[2]—a narrow definition which measures the proportion of finance functions that is carried out by the central departments and units of the finance ministry; and a broader definition which measures the proportion of functions carried out by the finance ministry and/or the subordinate agencies that report directly to it (for example, a national revenue authority, a debt management office or a public procurement agency). The analysis also draws a distinction between policy functions such as preparing the budget, making macroeconomic forecasts, analyzing fiscal policy scenarios and advising on options for the reform of tax policies; and functions that are largely operational such as preparing the government's accounts and financial reports, controlling the execution of the budget and managing the government's cash balances. Further details about the fragmentation indexes and the division between policy and operational activities can be found in appendix A, while the results of the statistical analysis are described below.

As indicated before, a process of devolving core public finance functions to different agencies and/or line ministries has been a common occurrence in many developed countries during the last 20–30 years, often reflecting technical/institutional specialization or the creation of more autonomous agencies with narrower technical mandates, for which there may be potential microeconomic efficiency gains.

In the case of low-income countries, an opposite phenomenon has occurred either as a result of a political decision to divide work among two or more central ministries or just due to ineffective coordination among CFAs.

There is no comprehensive theory behind the concentration or devolution of operational/policy functions in the public finance literature. However, it can be argued that some forms of specialization (for example, of operational functions) are consistent with theories originating from the New Institutional Economics (NIE) and New Public Management (NPM) which emphasize the growth of the culture of "managerialism" and accountability in government, and the importance of incentives for "managers to manage." Such theories had a considerable impact on the organization of government in advanced countries in the 1980s and 1990s, especially countries with an Anglophone, Scandinavian and U.S. tradition of public management. During this period, they were partly responsible for the devolution of many functions—especially operational functions—from central ministries of finance to spending ministries and subordinate agencies. As a result, one would predict that, in advanced countries, the concentration of these functions in the hands of the finance minister will have reduced significantly, though responsibility for policy functions is much less likely to have changed. In some advanced countries, the devolution of finance functions has been influenced by political considerations, in particular an effort by the head of state or prime minister to reduce the authority of the finance minister over economic and financial policy, by splitting the finance ministry into two or more parts.[3] Another important trend in the past 30 years has been the development of sophisticated ICT systems which enable the government to devolve routine operational tasks to spending agencies, while maintaining overall fiscal control. A useful analysis of these issues and trends in France, Germany, the United Kingdom and other developed countries is provided by Allen and Kohnert (2012).

Developing this hypothesis further, one might expect that—as discussed in chapter 2—as countries move from one stage of development to another, the concentration of CFAs would exhibit an inverted U-shape pattern such as that exhibited in figure 3.1. At low-income levels, countries often have highly "fragmented" CFAs in which control of public finances is divided among different institutions and/or political groups—often by heads of state who, deliberately or not deliberately, divide the authority of the finance minister in order to boost their own authority.[4] Dispersed manual systems of accounting, reporting and

Figure 3.1   Concentration of CFA Functions across Countries by Income Levels

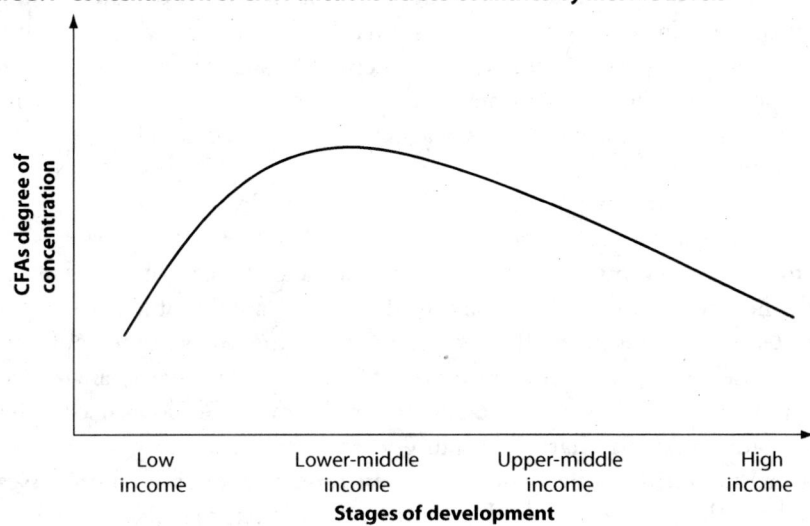

Source: World Bank data.

financial control tend to reinforce this phenomenon. As countries move to middle-income status, pressures to consolidate public finance functions within the finance ministry increase, often with the active encouragement of the International Monetary Fund (IMF) and World Bank.[5] There is a straightforward technological/capacity side to this, because a government needs a minimum level of both to build up the control mechanisms to effectively enforce consolidation. The more politicians worry about electoral competition and the more parties or groups are created, the more a head of government starts to focus on the importance of stabilizing the country's medium-term macroeconomic conditions and fiscal discipline, and therefore the more likely it is for a strong and concentrated CFA system to emerge. Policies such as integrating the budget and planning processes, bringing extra-budgetary funds within the budget, and merging government bank accounts within a treasury single account, are examples of this trend towards concentration.

As noted earlier, in advanced settings Public Financial Management (PFM) reforms may lead to less concentration and a broader distribution of functions as part of growing demand for organizational autonomy and discretion. In other words, as countries move to upper-middle-income and high-income country status, finance ministers are unlikely to relax their grip on central controls of the budget process, unless political conditions require them to do so. Even in the budget area, as noted above, the role of the finance ministry may change from directly operating the systems concerned to an oversight and monitoring function, while direct operations are transferred to line ministries and/or subordinate agencies responsible for treasury and procurement functions. Moreover, many CFA functions—such as macroeconomic forecasting, revenue and customs administration, and debt management—are not directly associated with the budget process. In many of these areas, finance ministers may delegate operational responsibility for the functions concerned to subordinate agencies under their supervision. The distribution of CFA functions may therefore increase, as the "managerial" culture spreads, new agencies are created, and further computerization takes place.

It is important to note, however, that these trends do not systematically apply to all countries in the same income-level groups. For example, the establishment of autonomous revenue and procurement agencies is also observed in some middle-income countries. And, similarly, there are examples of heavy concentration of CFA functions in the finance ministry in some low-income countries.

The causes and types of concentration of CFA functions may change as countries progress through various stages of development. At low-income levels, fragmentation may arise largely because finance ministries do not have (or are not given) sufficient political authority to exercise control of fiscal processes. At high-income levels, the broader distribution of functions may instead reflect the development of specialized finance functions, such as debt management and revenue administration for which an autonomous agency is better able to recruit and retain staff with the required skills, make use of specialized ICT systems, deliver high-quality services, and be held accountable for its performance. Some tentative evidence in support of this interesting inverted U-curve hypothesis is provided below, but the hypothesis needs to be tested by further empirical research.

An analysis of the CFA database is set out in the figures presented below. Figures 3.2 and 3.3 indicate that the allocation of roles and responsibilities for

Figure 3.2 CFA Concentration across Regions

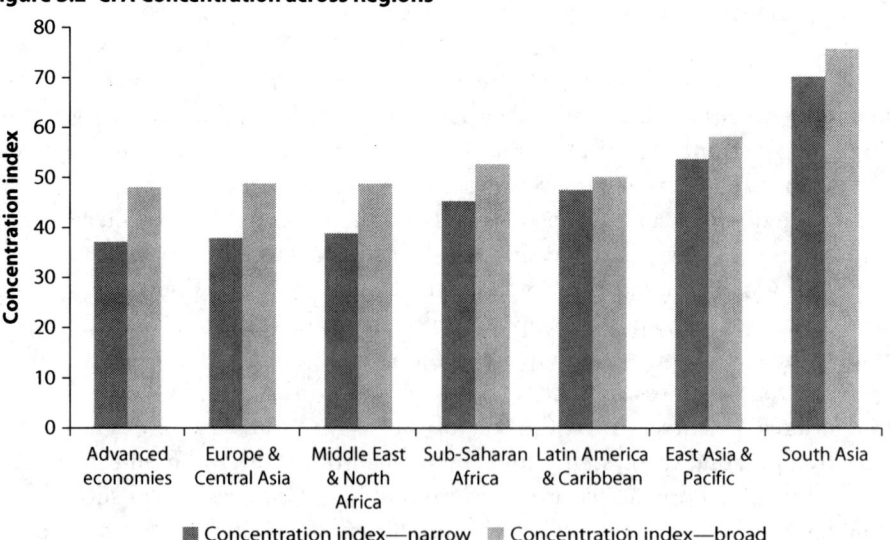

Source: World Bank data.

Figure 3.3 CFA Concentration across Country Income Groups

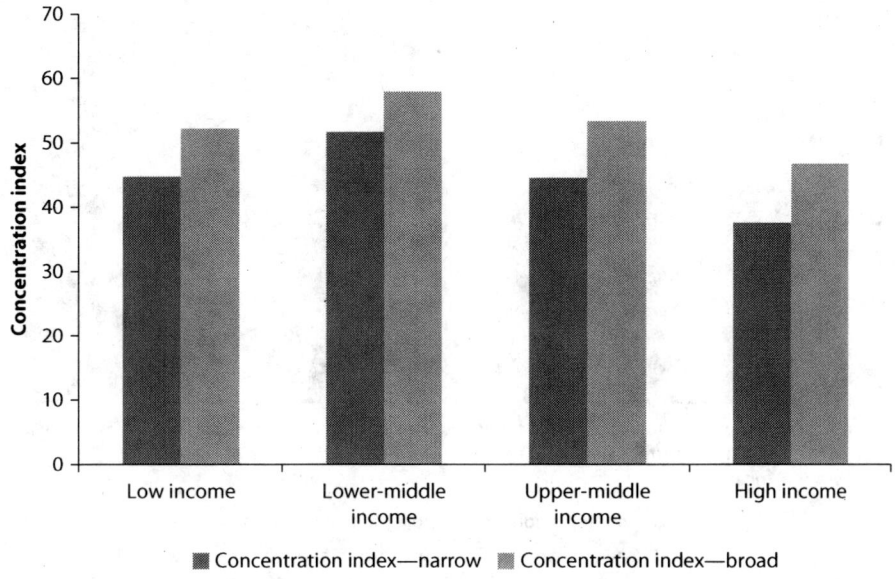

Source: World Bank data.

CFA functions among the finance ministry itself and other government agencies varies substantially across regions and country income groups.[6] Of the six regions studied, the Middle East and North Africa, and Europe and Central Asia[7] show the lowest levels of concentration, while South Asian countries show the highest ones[8]

In general, consistent with the inverted-U-shape hypothesis described above, advanced countries and lower-income countries have lower concentration ratios than middle-income countries. Nevertheless, these results have to be considered as tentative because of the limited country sample and composition, as well as the lack of empirical analysis behind the hypothesis.

Figure 3.4 shows that operational functions are in general less highly concentrated than policy functions, regardless of regional classification. Examples of operational functions are Treasury and Cash Management, and Civil Service Payment functions. Policy functions include Tax Policy Formulation and Legislation functions, among others (see table 3.1 for a complete list of both operational and policy functions of CFAs).

When comparing across country income groups, it is observed that in advanced countries the concentration index, narrowly defined, for policy functions is much higher than the concentration index for operational functions (see figure 3.5). The differences between operational and policy functions are relatively smaller in low-income and middle-income countries, though there is considerable variability among the sample. As expected, concentration among operational functions at high-income level decreases substantially, giving support to the U-curve hypothesis.

Figure 3.4 CFA Concentration of Policy and Operational Functions across Regions

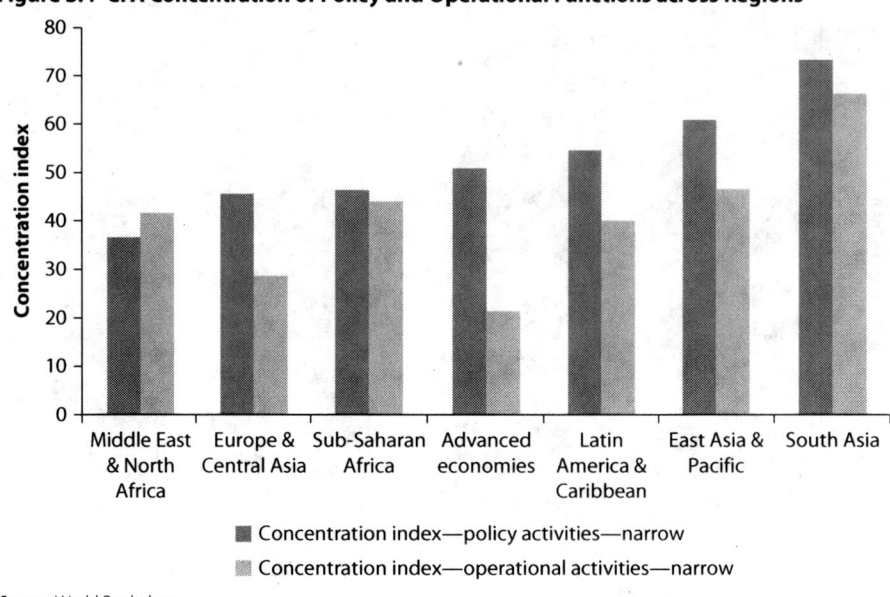

Source: World Bank data.

Table 3.1 Distribution of Scores for Each CFA Activity

Activity	Score mode	Frequency
Preparing forecasts and projections of macroeconomic indicators?	0	39.6
Preparing reports on macroeconomic and fiscal developments?	0	45.3
Analyzing and evaluating tax policy proposals, and preparing legislation?	0	56.6
Preparing the government's annual budget proposal submitted to the legislature?	0	73.6
Preparing the budget for development projects and capital investments?	0	43.4
Developing the framework for managing public investment projects and monitoring its implementation?	4	28.3
Managing government concessions and public-private partnerships?	4	34.0
Managing overseas aid, including negotiations with donors?	0	35.8
Preparing the government's strategy for domestic and external debt?	0	50.9
Establishing a framework for recording and regulating the financial assets and liabilities that are owned and managed by the state and monitoring the framework's implementation?	0	49.0
Developing a framework for managing expenditures, revenues, transfers, borrowing and other financial transactions of subnational government entities?	0	39.6
Managing the accounting, execution and control of the budget?	0	58.5
Forecasting and managing the government's requirements for cash?	0	60.4
Managing the government's banking arrangements?	0	52.8
Setting standards of accounting and financial reporting for government entities?	0	67.9

(table continues on next page)

Table 3.1 Distribution of Scores for Each CFA Activity *(continued)*

Activity	Score mode	Frequency
Defining the scope of internal audit procedures throughout government and setting standards for the application of internal audit by government entities?	0	43.4
Establishing policies and rules guiding public procurement and monitoring their implementation?	0	39.6
Undertaking procurement operations?	4	56.6
Establishing and managing the payroll system?	0	34.0
Establishing, monitoring and enforcing the regulatory framework for banks and other financial institutions?	4	58.5
Establishing a financial framework for managing and divesting state-owned enterprises and monitoring its implementation?	0	39.6
Collecting income taxes, VAT, sales taxes and other government revenues?	1	41.5
Enforcing customs' regulations (for example border controls) and collecting customs' duties?	1	37.4
Coordinating the government PFM reform strategy?	0	71.7

Source: CFA database.
Note: VAT = value-added tax; PFM = Public Financial Management.

Figure 3.5 CFA Concentration of Policy and Operational Functions across Income Groups

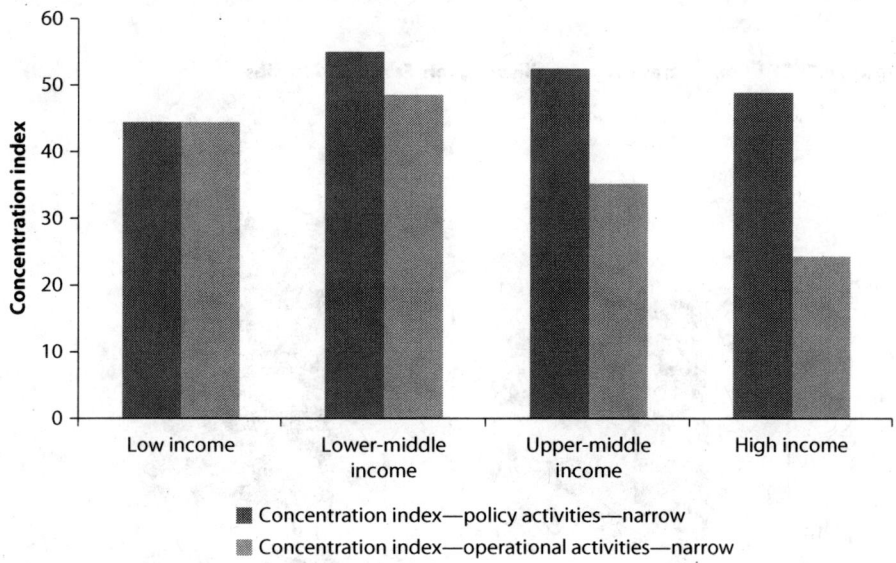

■ Concentration index—policy activities—narrow
■ Concentration index—operational activities—narrow

Source: World Bank data.

Figures 3.6 and 3.7 present relevant results for resource-rich countries and fragile states. In general, one would expect the concentration of CFA functions to be lower in resource-rich countries than in nonresource-rich countries for the following reason. Resource richness constitutes a potentially huge additional source of fiscal revenues—and fiscal risk and volatility—which is often managed

Figure 3.6 CFA Concentration in Resource-Rich and Non-Resource-Rich Countries

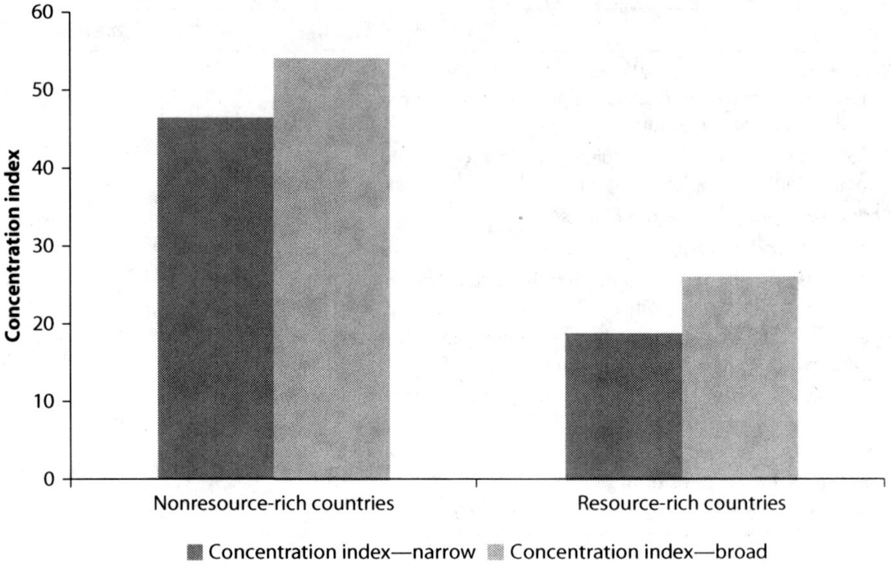

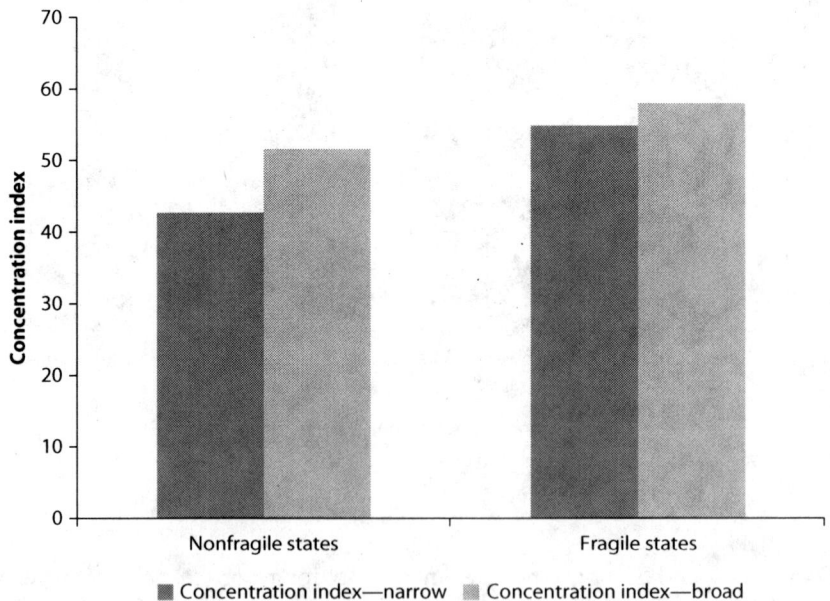

Source: World Bank data.
Note: Resource-rich countries are defined for this purpose as those for which the ratio of oil exports to gross domestic product (GDP) is higher or equal to 30 percent.

Figure 3.7 CFA Concentration in Fragile and Non-Fragile Countries

Source: World Bank data.
Note: Fragile states are defined as the countries on the World Bank's 2010 list of Low-income Countries under Stress (LICUS).

outside the central budget using special instruments such as sovereign wealth funds. In many resource-rich countries, the energy ministry and/or the national petroleum company also become a powerful source of financial influence and political patronage, thus weakening the role of the finance ministry as the primus inter pares of CFAs.

In the case of fragile states, the reverse is true. As discussed in a recent World Bank study (Fritz et al., 2011), there is often a unique opportunity in such countries to consolidate fiscal functions within the finance ministry due to the emergency status of public finances and the fragility of political groups, and because consolidation is usually agreed upon donors and recipient governments in order to avoid fragmentation so as to focus on the uses of the limited resources available. The data presented below provides tentative support for these hypotheses, and add to the inverted-U-shape hypothesis of concentration discussed above.

Table 3.1 shows the distribution of scores across countries for each of the 24 CFA activities: the mode is the most frequently recorded score with "0," indicating that the function is directly carried out by the ministry of finance, and it represents the highest level of concentration/consolidation. A score higher than "0" indicates that the function is carried out by other agencies and ministries with more autonomy vis-a-vis the finance ministry, or completely independent of the finance ministry. See appendix A for further details of the scoring methodology.

The frequency with which a score occurs is indicated in the second column. Although the most frequently recorded score is "0"[9]—indicating that there is complete concentration of that function at the finance ministry, the relative frequency shows a high variation: from 75.5 percent for "preparing the government's annual budget proposal submitted to the legislature" to 34.7 percent for "managing overseas aid, including negotiations with donors," the lower frequency number indicating a broader organizational distribution for such functions.

In general, the activities for which responsibility is most often spread to agencies and ministries independent of the finance ministry include the management of government concessions and PPPs, management of the regulatory framework for banks and other financial institutions, public investment management and the undertaking of procurement operations. This result is not surprising considering that these functions are more operational in character, involve an important interface between the government and the private sector, and are generally considered to require some degree of independence (or removal from political influence) that will strengthen their oversight and accountability, resulting in better outcomes for both the private sector and the government. Staff size is another important feature of CFAs. However, collection of data on staffing proved challenging,[10] and only a relatively small number of observations are available. The average number of people working in finance ministries, of the 22 countries for which data were obtained, is about 7,500. There is a huge variation in these numbers, mainly reflecting country population size, which range from 81 employees (Swaziland) to more than 110,000 employees (India). However, in some countries, these numbers are inflated by staff working in manpower-intensive occupations such as revenue and customs administration. In other countries, such functions are devolved to subordinate agencies, and would not appear in the staff numbers for the central finance ministry. When these factors are adjusted for, the average size of a central finance ministry is around 1,100 staff.[11] The number of CFA staff seems to reflect the size of the population, but does not seem to be affected by per capita income levels.

Only 10 of the questionnaires received included data on staff with a breakdown by gender. Thus, the sample is not representative of global and regional trends, but some interesting facts emerge. In Africa and the Middle East, female employees from the finance ministry are clearly in the minority, ranging from 10.4 percent to 35.9 percent of total employees in African countries and from 1.1 percent to 12.1 percent in the Middle East and North Africa. In Eastern Europe and Central Asia, female employees represent a larger portion: as high as 85 percent in Latvia and 78 percent in Slovenia (traditionally in this region, women have been employed extensively in accounting functions and other day-to-day operations). In all but one country,[12] female managers represented less than 4 percent of total staff.[13]

The use of ICT systems varies substantially across CFA institutions, as well as countries and regions. ICT is important to ensure the proper flow of information within a ministry, across ministries and to stakeholders external to government. It could be argued that countries that have email, use email and have an intranet are more likely to adopt management information systems than countries that do not, as such systems are typically dependent on email to keep officials informed and require knowledge and information to be centrally accessible.[14] Of the 30 countries that responded to the survey regarding use of ICT, 26 countries stated that they had an official email system, and 21 countries that they actively used official email as their primary means of communication. In some instances, however, the missions observed that ministry staff routinely uses personal email accounts or nonofficial email accounts to communicate. Of the total respondents, 20 countries (67 percent) have some form of intranet or internal knowledge exchange platform. Looking at the data outside of the ministries of finance, it is interesting to note that specialized agencies—such as tax, customs and procurement authorities—are more likely to have and use email, and have an intranet. In the case of central banks, for which there are six observations, all provide official email and use official email, and four have an intranet.

Notes

1. Of the 110 countries that were originally targeted, only 55 countries responded. Part 1 of the questionnaire, to which all countries replied, is designed to capture information on the organizational structure of CFAs on the basis of the 16 core functions described in table 1.1. Most disappointing were the response to Parts 2 and 3 of the questionnaire which covered staffing and ICT issues—only 22 countries responded to Part 2 and 30 countries to Part 3.

2. See appendix A.

3. Examples of advanced and middle-income countries with divided finance ministries are Australia, Brazil, Canada, France, Turkey and the United States.

4. As observed in chapter 2, there may be exceptions to this general principle. In some countries, presidents seek to make alliances with the finance minister in order to increase their authority and deal with fiscal problems that threaten to impoverish the country. An example of this phenomenon is Uganda during the 1990s. Of the countries covered by the CFA study, Rwanda provides another example of a strong finance minister supported by the president. Fragile states are another category where fiscal functions are often consolidated within a strong finance ministry, in this case often with support of the IMF and donors.

5. Many countries in Central and Eastern Europe went through this process in the 1990s after the breakdown of the former Soviet Union. Soviet-style central planning bureaus were dismantled, and central financial control systems reinforced. The goal of joining the European Union was a further incentive for these countries to consolidate finance functions, as they had to comply with the stringent financial conditions (on internal control, audit and public procurement) imposed by the *acquis communautaire*.

6. Andrews (2010) shows that countries that exhibit good outcomes can have very different governance structures, challenging the idea of one-best-way models of public financial management systems and government structures in general.

7. Using the World Bank regional classification, the Middle East and North Africa is considered as one region, and Europe and Central Asia is considered as another one.

8. It should be remembered that the small sample size is a limitation for such interregional comparisons. For the same reason, no analysis was performed to identify patterns among different administrative traditions, which are very likely to affect the structure of the CFAs.

9. A score higher than "0" indicates that activities are carried out by other agencies and ministries under progressively less "control" by the central finance ministry, or independently. See appendix B for further details of the scoring methodology.

10. As noted in chapter 2, the human resource data collected by the finance ministries covered by the case studies were of relatively poor quality. In some countries, the Human Resource department did not prepare even a basic consolidated list of staff members, their qualifications, and career record.

11. The sample size was too small to test whether or not there is a significant difference between the number of finance staff in Anglophone and Francophone countries. For example in the latter, many civil servants at the finance ministry are typically located

in line ministries and local authorities to undertake functions of accounting and financial control.

12. The exception is Moldova, where about 45 percent of female employees are employed as managers.

13. See also the discussion in chapter 2.

14. However, this study only includes a preliminary analysis of ICT capabilities in CFAs. A more detailed study of key information systems related issues would be necessary in the near future in order to highlight challenges and possible improvements.

CHAPTER 4

Main Lessons of the CFA Study

In this concluding chapter we briefly highlight the main lessons learned from the Central Finance Agency (CFA) study, as they may be relevant to the World Bank and other development partners who are supporting efforts in low-income countries to strengthen their CFAs and prepare Public Financial Management (PFM) reform strategies. It should be emphasized that, despite the relatively narrow range of issues discussed in the present report, the findings of the analysis have direct implications for much of the diagnostic and operational work undertaken at the Bank.[1]

The first and most important lesson is that a political economy analysis of CFAs is highly relevant—indeed essential—to the design and implementation of initiatives to strengthen them. The absence of understanding of how political economy factors influence the behavior of CFAs in a certain country is likely to result in decisions about the management of priorities and functions that are ineffective and may lead to the wasteful use of development resources.[2] In terms of its dialogue with country authorities, disregarding political economy factors affecting CFAs would lead to suboptimal decisions in operations and, ultimately, poor development outcomes.

It can further be noted that in many low-income countries, the fact that challenging PFM reforms affecting CFAs, such as medium-term expenditure framework (MTEF) implementation or Financial Management Information System (FMIS) introduction, are poorly implemented has deeper underlying political economy reasons than just lack of capacity, knowledge and experience of officials to manage change. Indeed, resistance to such reforms may be strong because public finance systems often act as a counterweight to centralized political power and rent-seeking incentives. The systems and processes that are in place usually serve an important political purpose as they are part of the infrastructure that maintains the status quo. Thus, there is often little space for changes that would alter the existing political order despite the technical rationale why such reforms would have a positive development impact. Some analyses of the factors associated with such PFM reforms conclude that weakness may stem from technical complexity, lack of capability and adequate change management strategies, and so on. However, in many cases, political economy factors may have been the predominant determinant behind unsatisfactory implementation scores.

An important implication of this finding is that political economy analysis should be undertaken when proposing new initiatives to strengthen PFM systems in the context of lending operations so that both technical and political viabilities are taken into consideration.[3] Many initiatives may be deemed sound at a technical level, and attractive for development partners in relation to their country programs and involvement with country clients, but too risky or uncertain from a political point of view. Thus, political economy analysis is of critical importance in strengthening CFAs by (a) placing PFM reform in the context of a wider development strategy; (b) exploring existing vulnerabilities explaining poor implementation of CFA reforms; (c) fostering best fit interventions, including issues of prioritization and sequencing of reform; and (d) sustaining and maintaining reform momentum.

Two further important lessons may be drawn: first, it would seem prudent to conduct an initial political economy analysis of a proposed intervention before too much investment and commitment is made by development partners; second, greater use of political economy analysis may lead to operations that disburse against performance results. Political economy analysis should not only be used as a filter, but throughout the preparation of a support operation, and during its implementation. Within the Bank, the new lending framework based on results, which links disbursements directly to outcomes achieved, constitutes an ideal framework to integrate the political economy analysis and focus on all the unexplained reasons behind ineffective functioning of CFAs. The present study has also shown that in many developing countries there are constraints on the extent to which it is possible to conduct an open dialogue of political economy issues with the Bank's government counterparts. Such discussions tend to touch on raw nerves and to meet resistance from country authorities. Even in countries in which circumstances permit explicit political economy analysis to be carried out, a nuanced approach is required. For example, in some countries, there may be opportunities for the Bank and other development agencies to invest in building up a continuing dialogue and long-term relationships of trust with leaders of the reform effort who are relatively open to difficult conversations about political relationships and constraints. Relationships of this kind are potentially important when the Bank is considering a new lending program that includes a significant number of CFA or PFM components, and where difficult judgments about the political and institutional feasibility of the various components need to be made.

In countries where an open dialogue with government counterparts can take place, it is important that the Bank and other donors make a larger investment in advising their client countries on change management strategies. Such advice goes well beyond the conventional focus on "capacity building," and should take full account of the constraints and potential blockages to reform that exist because of institutional disincentives to reform, political rivalries among government ministers, and so on. If a certain reform is likely to run into opposition because of resistance from line ministers or the head of state, strategies need to be developed to deal with such opposition, or the reform should not be embarked upon. Most developed countries have made extensive use of such change management strategies in implementing their reforms, but the analysis has been less systematically used in low-income countries. In expanding its work in this field the Bank should encourage broader participation in missions including staff outside the traditional Poverty Reduction and Economic Management (PREM) sector—for example, those with knowledge of human resource management.

In addition, more work is needed to develop nuanced and innovative approaches to strengthening CFAs. Approaches based on the best practice in developed countries have rightly been criticized as being of limited relevance in developing countries. As demonstrated by Andrews (2010) and others, "best fit," "good enough governance" and "second-best" solutions provide a better approach but need to take account of the institutional environment as well as technical conditions. Workable solutions often require political trade-offs as well as sound technical design. For example, some recent work by the Bank has proposed the "incentive compatible reforms" in Mongolian project selection (see Hasnain 2011).

The CFA study raises questions about the skills and experience of development staff who are expected to undertake political economy analysis. Some have specific skills in political science, and clearly such skills are desirable.[4] More important perhaps is the development of familiarity and knowledge of the countries concerned. Political economy conditions vary substantially from region to region, and even from country to country: what is feasible in China may not be so in Argentina or Nigeria.[5] The statistical database described in chapter 3 is a useful source of information and analysis of CFAs, but the Bank could invest in further work to extend the number of countries and topics covered, and the scope of the statistical analysis. The data provide some support for the inverted-U-shape hypothesis that CFAs may go through various stages of fragmentation during the country's evolution from low-income to high-income status. The database also provides useful information on the wide range of staff numbers working in central ministries of finance (ranging from less than 100 staff in some countries to several thousand staff in others), the gender breakdown and the use of information and communication technology (ICT) (including email) systems. The Bank should consider standardizing its collection of basic information on the functions, organizational structure, staffing, and ICT systems of CFAs. Such information is an essential ingredient of functional and organizational reviews of CFAs.[6]

Should consideration be given to extending existing diagnostic tools, notably the Public Expenditure and Financial Accountability (PEFA) assessment framework, to include questions on political economy issues? In principle, such an expansion of the PEFA methodology could be made, and might make it easier to apply the findings of PEFA assessments to undertake broader PFM reforms in developing countries. On the other hand, inclusion of an explicit political economy analysis in the questionnaire would heighten the political sensitivity of the results, and could further discourage the authorities from agreeing to the publication of PEFA assessments.[7] However, we recommend that the PEFA Steering Committee might want to consider this issue as part of a general review of the PEFA methodology, and as a way to institutionalize the collection of basic but relevant statistics. Extending the PEFA framework to include questions such as the number of staff, the gender balance, and the use of ICT systems in CFAs should be considered.

Finally, should the Bank and other donors consider creating new products, or modifying existing ones, such as Country Assistance Strategies (CASs) and Implementation Completion Reports (ICRs), on the basis of the analysis in this report? Certainly, existing tools should incorporate considerations about the political economy environment. More important, we suggest that a specific CFA toolkit could be developed—with characteristics of both a diagnostic tool and a set of guidelines—drawing on the principles of the Dressel-Brumby framework. The toolkit, which has an obvious association with the Bank's recently launched Program-for-Results financing instrument, would be designed to assist Bank missions in advising finance ministers on how to strengthen the capability of CFAs and to help transform the finance ministry into a center of excellence on public finance issues, much as central banks provide timely and technically competent work in the counterpart field of monetary and exchange rate policy. Based on our analysis in a number of developing countries, such a toolkit could well be in demand, especially from countries that are in the upper-low-income and middle-income categories. It would also help identify areas of PFM reform which are both technically feasible and not constrained by political economy factors as discussed in this report.

Table 4.1 below provides an illustrative outline of how the CFA toolkit might be constructed. Its full development requires further consultation within the Bank and with client country counterparts. Issues to note are as follows:

- This approach, as noted, is designed to strengthen the role of CFAs with the ministry of finance being considered as a center of excellence in developing strategies and policies for the efficient management of public finances, in an analogous way that the central bank is the preeminent authority on monetary and exchange rate policy. As discussed in chapter 1, the toolkit would assess a range of **internal** capabilities such as the organizational structure and staffing of the finance ministry and the extent to which **external** influences—such as the mandate and political authority of the president and the minister of planning, or the role of the legislature—dilute or constrain the minister's ability to manage public finances effectively.
- The CFA toolkit would establish a baseline of capabilities (illustrated in the second column of table 4.1) and a set of objectives or targets to be achieved (the sixth column).

Table 4.1 Performance Framework for Analyzing the Capabilities of a Ministry of Finance (Illustrative Outline)

Capabilities	Description	Establishing baseline of capabilities	Availability of technical solution (examples)	Political economy challenges (examples)	Anticipated outcomes and results
1. Internal					
Allocation of functions	16 CFA functions/24 activities.	Map of functional responsibilities. Extent of overlap with responsibilities of other CFAs.	Functional and organizational review of the MoF, and its subordinate agencies.	Overlap of responsibilities with presidency/ministry of planning. Dual budget.	Revised map of de facto functional responsibilities. Revisions to public finance law.
Top management structure	Ministers, deputy ministers, director-generals.	Core competencies. Formal duties and responsibilities. Reporting arrangements. Appointment/removal.	Review of top management structures included in the functional review.	Resistance of finance minister to changes that dilute his detailed day-to-day control.	Revised organizational chart of the MoF, and revised job descriptions.
Attraction and retention of staff	Middle managers, junior staff, professional accountants, economists, finance specialists, technical consultants and advisors, support staff.	Staffing numbers in MoF. Core skills and competencies. Duties and responsibilities. Turnover rates. Career development. Use of international technical consultant. Access to education.	Review of HR functions—included in functional and organizational review of MoF. The ministry should be compared to the highest performing local public institution (for example, the Central Bank) and international standards.	Proposed changes may conflict with application of civil service-wide standards for recruitment and retention of staff. Existence of large number of donor-financed consultants in line positions.	HR Strategy and Implementation Plan. Each staff position would have clear Terms of Reference (TORs); learning program and young professional scheme; use of technical consultants minimized; plan for reducing turnover rates.
Performance management	All MoF staff, public sector unions.	Use of performance standards within MoF. Impact of good/poor performance on pay, career development, and so on.	Review of existing scheme and how indicators are established; who undertakes assessments; if private sector alternatives exist to provide more efficient service.	Limited ownership by senior managers; reluctance to use performance evaluation results to determine pay and career development; limited freedom for MoF to introduce a revised scheme independent of Civil Service Ministry.	Revised scheme. Civil service should be reassured that merit-based performance will provide opportunities for growth and provide job security, and that steady good performance will help reduce the need to outsource.

(table continues on next page)

Table 4.1 Performance Framework for Analyzing the Capabilities of a Ministry of Finance (Illustrative Outline) *(continued)*

Capabilities	Description	Establishing baseline of capabilities	Availability of technical solution (examples)	Political economy challenges (examples)	Anticipated outcomes and results
Change management	Mechanisms for building consensus on need for reorganization, and facilitating the design and implementation of proposed reforms.	Assessment of existing mechanisms within MoF. Leadership by minister and top managers of MoF. Review of past reform results.	Organizational review of MoF to include recommendations on change management strategy. Assessment of experience of outside/international comparators. Review appropriate mechanisms for staff consultations.	Opposition to reforms by MoF's senior managers and staff. Strong internal incentives among staff to preserve existing arrangements. Limited opportunities to compensate losers.	Change management strategy linked to a results framework. Establishment of a reform coordination unit with political power to enact reforms.
Use of internal ICT systems	MoF website on which official reports are posted, and an email system.	ICT available, such as email, intranet and access to personal computer ICT uptake ICT systems in place for PFM, for example., IFMIS, database on ODA.	Review of ICT systems linked to functional and organizational review of MoF. Access to information mandates should be considered in the context of an analysis of mechanisms for exchanging information.	Resistance of senior managers and staff to share information through official websites and email systems; special interests that impede ICT developments and favor local suppliers/platforms; lack of ability to secure ICT assets; unwillingness of government to invest in ICT architecture.	Technical solutions are relatively straightforward: can be included in an ICT development plan. Political economy challenges likely to be much more significant. ICT systems without political will to operate them and weak staff preparation will not lead to the desired results.
2. External					
Center of government (CoG)	Formal and informal role of CoG (President, Prime Minister, planning ministry and council of ministers) other than the MoF in decision making on budget and other finance functions.	Formal map of roles and responsibilities of CFAs. Influence of CoG on key finance decisions and day-to-day operations of MoF.	Existing diagnostic instruments (for example., PEFA) may provide some information; but need to be supplemented by additional assessments.	Inefficient distribution of responsibilities among key actors. Informal rules predominate. Large discretion for President to decide budget allocations without MoF approval.	May be some scope for clarifying roles and responsibilities, but fundamental changes to informal "rules of the game" may be limited.

(table continues on next page)

Table 4.1 Performance Framework for Analyzing the Capabilities of a Ministry of Finance (Illustrative Outline) *(continued)*

Capabilities	Description	Establishing baseline of capabilities	Availability of technical solution (examples)	Political economy challenges (examples)	Anticipated outcomes and results
Line ministries	Clarity of roles and responsibilities of MoF and line ministries in relation to budget preparation and execution.	Existing distribution of formal responsibilities between MoF and line ministries. Indicators of efficiency of delivery of key public services.	Recommendations for clarifying roles and responsibilities.	Powerful line ministers who secure large budget allocations through informal mechanisms, for example., patronage of the President.	Clarification of roles and responsibilities as defined in budget law, but this may not change the informal rules and patronage arrangements.
Subordinate agencies of the MoF	Agencies delivering core finance functions such as revenue collection, procurement and debt management. Agencies formally report to MoF, but have independence on day-to day operations.	Formal allocation of responsibilities between MoF and agencies. Supervisory role of the minister of finance. Internal governance arrangements for subordinate agencies. Transparency, consistency and timeliness of financial reports produced by agencies.	Good practice models for managing agencies, based on international experience.	Agency heads enjoy patronage of President, and are directly appointed by him. *De facto* limitations on oversight role of finance minister. Lack of transparency in agency operations and financial reports; evidence of serious corruption in revenue collection.	Enhanced governance regime/ performance evaluation framework for the agencies. Reforms may have limited impact because of political economy constraints.
Legislature	Primary responsibility of the legislature is to approve the annual budget, and provide oversight of budget execution.	Formal powers of legislature as provided in constitution and budget laws. Internal mechanisms (for example., committee structures) within legislature to scrutinize the budget, financial reports and audit reports. Technical skills in budget analysis. Transparency and timeliness of parliamentary procedures and oversight.	Technical proposals to strengthen internal rules and procedures of legislature.	Legislature is a rubber-stamping operation, with limited powers to amend the draft budget, and no independent powers of oversight.	May be limited opportunities to strengthen existing arrangements in the short to medium term, except for minor technical changes.

(table continues on next page)

Table 4.1 Performance Framework for Analyzing the Capabilities of a Ministry of Finance (Illustrative Outline) *(continued)*

Capabilities	Description	Establishing baseline of capabilities	Availability of technical solution (examples)	Political economy challenges (examples)	Anticipated outcomes and results
Civil society	Several civil society organizations (CSOs) have a formal role in preparing the national development plan and annual budget, through participation in sector working parties (SWPs).	Modalities of engagement between the finance ministry, line ministries and CSOs. Effectiveness of formal CSO interfaces. Technical expertise to challenge experts in finance ministry on budget allocations, and so on. Existence within finance ministry of a unit with responsibility for CSO outreach. Availability of budget/finance reports to CSOs.	Proposals to strengthen capacity of CSOs to monitor budget execution; establish formal interfaces between the finance ministry and CSOs (if none exist), based on international experience; strengthen strategic communications and outreach.	Relations between the finance ministry and CSOs are largely formal; in practice, CSOs have limited opportunities and resources to influence budget outcomes.	May be limited opportunities in the short to medium term to strengthen capacity of CSOs to influence policy decisions on the budget.
Donor Partners	Sector-based, in-country donor working groups on budget and national development plan; PFM reform coordination group, chaired by MoF, includes donor representation; donors also participate in SWPs.	Level of direct donor involvement in budget preparation and other CFA operations. Scope of externally financed budget support. Existence of consistent plans and forward estimates of ODA. Past results on PFM reform.	Bring ODA database and forward estimates into line with best practice in LICs. Review MoF's role in managing ODA, and leading the PFM reform strategy.	Relations between donors and country authorities are inherently political. MoF is weak: PFM reform strategy is largely donor driven. Coordination among donors is very weak, despite existence of PFM reform strategy.	Strengthening the capability of the MoF to engage with donor partners is likely to lead to more robust dialogue and better understanding of reform challenges and solutions.

Note: MoF = Ministry of Finance; HR = human resource; ICT = information and communication technology; PFM = Public Financial Management; IFMIS = Integrated Financial Management Information System; ODA = official development assistance; PEFA = Public Expenditure and Financial Accountability; LICs = low-income countries.

- Unlike in the PEFA system, where specific quantitative criteria have been developed, the assessment of capabilities, and the extent of political economy constraints, is perhaps more a matter of the opinion and judgment of the assessor. There are, however, quantitative indicators[8]—such as the number and qualifications of professional staff, turnover rates, the use of websites and other ICT systems, and so on—that could be used to support the analysis. Indeed, we argued earlier that the Bank's country units should be encouraged to collect such data on a routine basis.

- The CFA toolkit would complement existing technical instruments such as PEFA which do not include questions on organizational structures, staffing levels or other aspects of capability.

- Since, for reasons discussed earlier, the political consensus is many "limited access" developing countries is to use budget systems to safeguard existing political structures, the opportunities for reform are more limited than in open-access countries. It would similarly be more challenging to utilize the PforR framework in such countries. However, one could conceive disbursements based on results that "move the dial" on the reform trajectory: for example, as noted in the framework paper, by using a coalition of parties to set in motion a set of reforms, or to move ahead with an "open budget" agenda by using active citizen engagement on budget issues.

- A toolkit along the lines outlined above would be useful first in describing and analyzing the political economy factors that influence the behavior of CFAs. However, an additional effort should be made, on the basis of such analysis, to help countries develop a system of incentives that would enable them to select the best politically feasible reform options and put them into a proper sequence, even when these may not always be the first best technical solutions.

Notes

1. A recent World Bank report notes that "in order to improve development effectiveness, governance and political economy diagnostics should become integral to preparing and implementing Bank strategies and operations." Fritz, Kaiser, and Levy (2009, vii).

2. This lesson is fully consistent with the findings of the recently issued IEG-GAC evaluation report which indicates a clear relationship between the usage of analytical tools in political economy and the governance responsiveness in Bank projects. IEG Working Paper, 2011/4.

3. The 2001 IEG-GAC evaluation report concludes that political economy analysis is still thinly and inconsistently applied at the Bank and could benefit from higher standards of quality and methodological rigor, better political economy operational guidelines, better political economy inputs into economic and sector work (ESW) and CAS, and more downstream support at the project level. IEG Working Paper, 2011/4.

4. The World Bank's Community of Practice on Political Economy has created a database that provides access to specialists with expertise in different regions and sectors.

5. For example, the CFA study of Nicaragua benefited greatly from the deep knowledge of the team leader of the political and financial environment in countries in the region, which enabled the team to develop a tailored set of recommendations which closely matched the expectations and requirements of the authorities.

6. In addition to the CFA case studies for Ghana, Rwanda, the Republic of Yemen, and so on reviewed in the present report, such organizational/functional reviews have been carried out by the Bank and International Monetary Fund (IMF) in countries such as Indonesia, Nicaragua, and Peru; a recent request has also been received from the authorities in the Philippines.

7. According to Lawson and Folscher (2011), the publication rate for PEFA assessment reports finalized in 2009 and 2010 was less than 40 percent.

8. The database described in chapter 3 includes several such indicators.

BIBLIOGRAPHY

Allen, R. 2008. "Reforming Fiscal Institutions: The Elusive Art of the Budget Advisor." *OECD Journal of Budgeting* 8 (3): 1–9.

Allen, R., and P. Kohnert. 2012. The Anatomy of the Ministry of Finance. Mimeo. Washington, DC: International Monetary Fund.

Andrews, M. 2010. "Good Governance Means Different Things in Different Countries." *Governance* 23 (1): 7.

Dener, C., J. A. Watkins, and W. L. Dorotinsky. 2011. *Financial Management Information Systems, 25 Years of World Bank Experience on What Works and What Doesn't.* A World Bank Study. Washington, DC: World Bank.

Dressel, B., and J. Brumby. 2009. "Enhancing the Capabilities of Central Finance Agencies: From Diagnosis to Action." Framework Paper, World Bank, Washington, DC.

Fritz, V., E. Hedger, and A. P. Filhao Lopes. 2011. "Strengthening Public Financial Management in Postconflict Countries." *Economic Premise* 54, World Bank.

Fritz, V., K. Kaiser, and B. Levy. 2009. *Problem-Driven Governance and Political Economy Analysis.* Washington, DC: World Bank.

Hasnain, Z. 2011. "Incentive Compatible Reforms: The Political Economy of Public Investments in Mongolia." Policy Research Working Paper 5667, World Bank, Washington, DC.

Hedger, E., and A. Z. Kizilbash. 2007. "Reforming Public Financial Management When the Politics Aren't Right: A Proposal." ODI Opinion 89, November.

Lawson, A., and A. Folscher. 2011. Evaluation of PEFA Programme 2004-2010 & Development of Recommendations beyond 2011. Final Report submitted by Fiscus and Mokoro to the PEFA Steering Committee, July 2011.

North, A., J. Wallis, S. Webb, and B. Weingast. 2007. "Limited Access Orders in the Developing World: A New Approach to the Problems of Development." World Bank Policy Research Working Paper 4359, World Bank, Washington, DC.

Poole, A. 2011. "How to Notes: Political Economy Analysis at Sector and Project Level." GAC in Projects, World Bank, Washington, DC.

Von Hagen, J. 2005. "Budgeting Institutions and Public Spending." In *Fiscal Management*, edited by Anwar A. Shah. Washington, DC: World Bank.

Wanna, J., and L. Jensen. 2010. *The Reality of Budgetary Reform in OECD Nations: Trajectories and Consequences.* Cheltenham: Edward Elgar Publishing.

Wanna, J., L. Jensen, and J. De Vries. 2003. *Controlling Public Expenditure: The Changing Roles of Central Budget Agencies—Better Guardians?* Cheltenham: Edward Elgar Publishing.

Questionnaire, Database, and Indexes

This appendix describes the questionnaire that has been used (attached at the end of the document) to compile the Central Finance Agency (CFA) database and the construction of the fragmentation index. As described in chapter 3 of this report, the database was used to compare and contrast the structure of CFAs and the distribution of central finance functions among various ministries and agencies of government. As explained below the worldwide sample includes a wide range of low-, lower-middle-, upper-middle and high-income countries.

The questionnaire comprises three sections. The first section called "Functions Questions" is designed to capture the distribution of 16 core CFA functions, subdivided into 24 activities, across ministries and agencies within a country. For each function, the survey asks about which agency has the primary responsibility for carrying out the function concerned, and whether there is any overlap or duplication among agencies in the assignment of this role and corresponding responsibilities. The survey also differentiates between the functions where the policy-making component is prominent and the functions that are more operational in nature, as presented in table A.1.

Table A.1 Central Finance Functions and Policy (P) and Operational (O) Activities

Function	Activity	P/O
Macroeconomic forecasting, analysis and fiscal policy	Preparing forecasts and projections of macroeconomic indicators	O
	Preparing reports on macroeconomic and fiscal developments	O
Tax policy	Analyzing and evaluating tax policy proposals, and preparing legislation	P
Budget preparation and analysis	Preparing the government's annual budget proposal submitted to the legislature	P
	Preparing the budget for development projects and capital investments	P
Public investment management	Developing the framework for managing public investment projects and monitoring its implementation	P
	Managing government concessions and public-private partnerships	O
Aid and debt management	Managing overseas aid, including negotiations with donors	O
	Preparing the government's strategy for domestic and external debt	P

(table continues on next page)

Table A.1 Central Finance Functions and Policy (P) and Operational (O) Activities *(continued)*

Function	Activity	P/O
Financial assets and liabilities	Establishing a framework for recording and regulating the financial assets and liabilities that are owned and managed by the state and monitoring the framework's implementation	P
Intergovernmental fiscal relations	Developing a framework for managing expenditures, revenues, transfers, borrowing and other financial transactions of subnational government entities	P
Treasury and cash management	Managing the accounting, execution and control of the budget	O
	Forecasting and managing the government's requirements for cash	O
	Managing the government's banking arrangements	O
Accounting and reporting	Setting standards of accounting and financial reporting for government entities	P
Internal audit	Defining the scope of internal audit procedures throughout government, and setting standards for the application of internal audit by government entities	P
Public procurement	Establishing policies and rules guiding public procurement and monitoring their implementation	P
	Undertaking procurement operations	O
Civil service pay	Establishing and managing the payroll system	O
Financial sector regulation	Establishing, monitoring and enforcing the regulatory framework for banks and other financial institutions	P
Financial framework for managing SOEs	Establishing a financial framework for managing and divesting state owned enterprises and monitoring its implementation	P
Revenue and customs administration	Collecting income taxes, VAT, sales taxes and other government revenues	O
	Enforcing customs' regulations (for example, border controls) and collecting customs' duties	O
PFM reform coordination	Coordinating the government PFM reform strategy	P

Note: SOEs = State Owned Enterprises; VAT = value added tax.

The second section named "Staffing Questions" is designed to collect human resource information for CFAs. The staffing questions cover issues such as staff size, staff composition, gender balance, and turnover ratios. The third section called "IT Questions" includes questions concerning the use of information and communications technology (ICT) and internal email systems within CFAs.

The database includes responses from 55 countries, out of 110 countries that were initially targeted. The sample of countries focused largely on low-income countries (LICs) and low middle-income countries (LMICs), but some eight high-income countries were also included to provide benchmarks against which the low- and middle-income countries can be compared. The percentage of Sub-Saharan countries is the highest among the regions. Table A.2 gives a breakdown of the countries included in the sample by region and income group and table A.3 provides the list of questionnaire respondents.

Table A.2 Database Composition

Region	Countries	Percentage
Advanced Economies	6	11.32
East Asia & Pacific	6	11.32
Europe & Central Asia	7	13.21
Latin America & Caribbean	5	9.43
Middle East & North Africa	5	9.43
South Asia	3	5.66
Sub-Saharan Africa	21	39.62
High income	8	15.09
Upper-middle income	18	33.96
Lower-middle income	15	28.3
Low income	12	22.64

Source: World Bank data.

Table A.3 Questionnaire Respondents

Afghanistan	Latvia	Solomon Islands
Australia	Lebanon	South Africa
Belarus	Malawi	Sri Lanka
Benin	Malaysia	Sudan
Botswana	Mauritania	Swaziland
Brazil	Mauritius	Sweden
Cameroon	Mexico	Syrian Arab Republic
Cape Verde	Moldova	Tajikistan
Chad	Mongolia	Tanzania
Chile	Mozambique	Togo
Egypt, Arab Rep.	New Zealand	Tonga
France	Nicaragua	Uganda
Gabon	Niger	United Kingdom
Gambia, The	Poland	United States
Germany	Russian Federation	West Bank and Gaza
Ghana	Rwanda	Yemen, Rep.
Haiti	São Tomé and Principe	Zimbabwe
India	Sierra Leone	
Jordan	Slovenia	

In general, survey respondents found the first section relatively straightforward to complete, although only about half of the countries approached completed the questionnaire. The second and the third section proved challenging as access to even quite basic information on staffing issues and use of ICT is often limited and not available on request from finance ministries and other CFAs. As a result, not many lessons can be drawn from these portions of the survey.

One of the main purposes of the survey was to analyze the degree of concentration of central finance functions. For the purposes of the study, finance functions are considered centralized if they are performed primarily by the

Ministry of Finance (MoF) or equivalent. Finance functions are considered less centralized if they are performed by a subordinate agency of the MoF or by a separate ministry or another government institution, such as the central bank.

In order to capture the degree of concentration, survey respondents were asked to provide a score on the basis of how removed the function is from the MoF. The scoring methodology is described in table A.4. The observation is scored 0 if the finance ministry is the only institution performing the function. The observation is scored 1 when a subordinate agency of the finance ministry takes a lead role in performing the function, with or without the participation of the finance ministry as a secondary agency. If the MoF and/or one of its subordinate agencies are the primary agencies with or without other agencies and ministries, and there is a secondary participation of other agencies and ministries, the function receives a score of 2. The observation is scored 3 if the function is performed by another agency or ministry and the MoF and/or its subordinate agency is considered to perform the function secondarily. Finally, if neither the MoF nor one of its subordinate agencies performs the function primarily or secondarily, the activity is scored 4. Two additional scores are included in table A.4 to capture when a function does not exist or is under development and not systematically carried out (scored a 5), or when the function does exist but it is unclear which ministry or agency is responsible (scored a 6).[1]

Finally, two concentration indexes were calculated to capture the intensity of the finance ministry's role in carrying out central finance functions. These indexes distinguish between countries in which the central departments and units of the finance ministry are directly responsible for carrying out core finance functions, and countries where the finance ministry also

Table A.4 Scoring Methodology

Score	Primary agency	Secondary agency
0	MoF	.
1	Subordinate agency of the MoF	.
1	Subordinate agency of the MoF	MoF
2	MoF	Other
2	MoF and subordinate agency of the MoF	Other
2	Subordinate agency of the MoF	Other
2	MoF and/or subordinate agency of the MoF, and other	Other
3	Other	MoF
3	Other	Subordinate agency of the MoF
4	Other	Other
5	Activity does not exist, under development or not systematically carried out.	
6	Activity does exist, but it is unclear which ministry or agency is responsible for it.	

Source: World Bank data.
Note: MoF = Ministry of Finance.

plays a key role, but delegates some functions to subordinate agencies which may be given a substantial degree of operational independence on a day-to-day basis but are fully accountable to the finance minister. Thus, the *narrow concentration index* is computed as the number of finance ministry functions rated 0 (carried out uniquely by the MoF) over the total number of activities reduced by the number of scored 5 and 6 (functions that do not exist, or for which there is no clarity about the responsibility). More formally:

$$\text{Concentration index} = \left(\frac{\sum_1^n A_i}{n-p} \right) \times 100$$

where A is an activity undertaken by the finance ministry, n is the total number of activities, p is the number of activities rated 5 or 6 and i is the subscript indentifying the index definition. Thus, a higher index value will reflect a CFA system more concentrated in the finance ministry. Similar indices have been computed separately for policy and operational functions. The *broad concentration index* is computed in the same way, but A now includes functions (both operational and policy) that have been scored 0 or 1 (carried out primarily by a subordinate agency of the MoF, with or without the contribution of the MoF). This allowed the task team to explore if concentration was greater amongst the former or the latter.

CFA Questionnaire

Country name:
1. Function Questions
Score Methodology:
0. Function is performed by the country's finance ministry.
1. Function is carried out primarily by a subordinate agency of the finance ministry with or without the secondary participation of the finance ministry.
2. Function is primarily performed primarily by the finance ministry and/or one of its subordinate agencies and secondarily by other government ministries or agencies that are not under the supervision of the finance ministry.
3. Function is primarily performed by other government ministries and secondarily by the finance ministry.
4. Function is performed by government ministries or agencies that are not under the supervision of the finance ministry.
5. Function does not exist, is still under development or is not systematically applied.
6. Function does exist, but it is unclear which ministry or agency is responsible for it.

(continues on next page)

CFA Questionnaire *(continued)*

No.	For each of the questions below please answer the following: which ministry or agency is responsible for?	Function	Name(s) of primary ministry or agency responsible for the function (if possible, please also specify name of unit/ department/ sector within the ministry)	Name(s) of secondary ministry or agency responsible for the function (if possible, please also specify name of unit/ department/ sector within the ministry)	Score (0–6)	If the score is 6, please explain why?	If the function is performed by more than 1 ministry/ agency, is there an overlap between the responsibilities of the ministries/ agencies that share the function?
1.a	Preparing forecasts and projections of macroeconomic indicators?	Macroeconomic forecasting, analysis and fiscal policy					
1.b	Preparing reports on macroeconomic and fiscal developments?						
2	Analyzing and evaluating tax policy proposals, and preparing legislation?	Tax policy					
3.a	Preparing the government's annual budget proposal submitted to the legislature?	Budget preparation and analysis					
3.b	Preparing the budget for development projects and capital investments?						
4.a	Developing the framework for managing public investment projects and monitoring its implementation?	Public investment management					
4.b	Managing government concessions and public-private partnerships?						
5.a	Managing overseas aid, including negotiations with donors?	Aid and debt management					
5.b	Preparing the government's strategy for domestic and external debt?						

(continues on next page)

CFA Questionnaire *(continued)*

No.	For each of the questions below please answer the following: which ministry or agency is responsible for?	Function	Name(s) of primary ministry or agency responsible for the function (if possible, please also specify name of unit/ department/ sector within the ministry)	Name(s) of secondary ministry or agency responsible for the function (if possible, please also specify name of unit/ department/ sector within the ministry)	Score (0–6)	If the score is 6, please explain why?	If the function is performed by more than 1 ministry/ agency, is there an over-lap between the responsi-bilities of the ministries/ agencies that share the func-tion?
6	Establishing a framework for recording and regu-lating the financial assets and liabilities that are owned and managed by the state and monitor-ing the framework's implementation?	Financial assets and liabilities					
7	Developing a frame-work for manag-ing expenditures, revenues, transfers, borrowing and other financial transactions of subnational govern-ment entities?	Intergovern-mental fiscal relations					
8.a	Managing the accounting, execu-tion and control of the budget?	Treasury and cash management					
8.b	Forecasting and managing the gov-ernment's require-ments for cash?						
8.c	managing the gov-ernment's banking arrangements?						
9	Setting standards of accounting and financial reporting for government entities?	Accounting and reporting					

(continues on next page)

CFA Questionnaire *(continued)*

No.	For each of the questions below please answer the following: which ministry or agency is responsible for?	Function	Name(s) of primary ministry or agency responsible for the function (if possible, please also specify name of unit/ department/ sector within the ministry)	Name(s) of secondary ministry or agency responsible for the function (if possible, please also specify name of unit/ department/ sector within the ministry)	Score (0–6)	If the score is 6, please explain why?	If the function is performed by more than 1 ministry/ agency, is there an over-lap between the responsi-bilities of the ministries/ agencies that share the func-tion?
10	Defining the scope of internal audit procedures throughout govern-ment, and setting standards for the application of inter-nal audit by govern-ment entities?	Internal audit					
11.a	Establishing policies and rules guiding public procurement and monitoring their implementation?	Public procurement					
11.b	Undertaking procurement operations?						
12	Establishing and managing the payroll system?	Civil service pay					
13	Establishing, monitoring and enforcing the regulatory frame-work for banks and other financial institutions?	Financial sector regulation					
14	Establishing a financial framework for managing and divesting state owned enterprises and monitoring its implementation?	Financial framework for managing SOEs					

(continues on next page)

CFA Questionnaire *(continued)*

No.	For each of the questions below please answer the following: which ministry or agency is responsible for?	Function	Name(s) of primary ministry or agency responsible for the function (if possible, please also specify name of unit/ department/ sector within the ministry)	Name(s) of secondary ministry or agency responsible for the function (if possible, please also specify name of unit/ department/ sector within the ministry)	Score (0–6)	If the score is 6, please explain why?	If the function is performed by more than 1 ministry/ agency, is there an over-lap between the responsi-bilities of the ministries/ agencies that share the func-tion?
15.a	Collecting income taxes, VAT, sales taxes and other government revenues?	Revenue and customs administration					
15.b	Enforcing customs' regulations (for example, border controls) and collecting customs' duties?						
16	Coordinating the government PFM reform strategy?	PFM reform coordination					
17	Please list any additional functions performed by the main finance minis-try but not included in the list above.	Nonidentified functions					
18	List the minis-ters (or minister equivalents) and ministerial portfo-lios responsible for the functions listed above.	Ministerial portfolios					

2. Staffing Questions						

Please answer questions 19–22 for the ministries/agencies listed below and, whenever possible, for any additional primary ministries/agencies listed in the previous section of the questionnaire.

No.	Question	Category	Ministry of Finance	Tax Authority	Customs Authority	Public Pro-curement Agency	Ministry of Economic Planning (or equivalent)
19.a	What is the total number of people working within the ministry/agency?	Staff size					

(continues on next page)

CFA Questionnaire *(continued)*

No.	Question	Category	Ministry of Finance	Tax Authority	Customs Authority	Public Procurement Agency	Ministry of Economic Planning (or equivalent)
19.b	What is the total number of people working within the headquarters of the ministry/agency?						
20.a	What is the total number of employees in the headquarters of the ministry/agency holding at least an undergraduate (bachelor) university degree?	Staff composition					
20.b	What is the total number of employees in the headquarters of the ministry/agency holding a postgraduate (Master, PhD) degree?						
21.a	What is the number of women working within the headquarters of the ministry/agency?	Gender balance					
21.b	What is the number of women within the headquarters of the ministry/agency who work at a higher-ranking/managerial position (that is, budget director or equivalent) within the finance ministry?						
22	What is the percentage of nonretiring headquarters employees that left their position in the last year?	Turnover ratio					

Additional ministries/agencies:			Ministry/agency 6	Ministry/agency 7	Ministry/agency 8	Ministry/agency 9	Ministry/agency 10
			Name:	Name:	Name:	Name:	Name:
19.a	What is the total number of people working within the ministry/agency?	Staff size					
19.b	What is the total number of people working within the headquarters of the ministry/agency?						

(continues on next page)

CFA Questionnaire *(continued)*

No.	Question	Category	Ministry of Finance	Tax Authority	Customs Authority	Public Procurement Agency	Ministry of Economic Planning (or equivalent)
20.a	What is the total number of employees in the headquarters of the ministry/agency holding at least an undergraduate (bachelor) university degree?	Staff composition					
20.b	What is the total number of employees in the headquarters of the ministry/agency holding a postgraduate (Master, PhD) degree?						
21.a	What is the number of women working within the headquarters of the ministry/agency?	Gender balance					
21.b	What is the number of women within the headquarters of the ministry/agency who work at a higher ranking/managerial position (that is, budget director or equivalent) within the finance ministry?						
22	What is the percentage of nonretiring headquarters employees that left their position in the last year?	Turnover ratio					
3. IT Questions							
Please answer questions 23–24 for the ministries/agencies listed below and, whenever possible, for any additional primary ministries/agencies listed in the previous section of the questionnaire.							

No.	Question	Category	Ministry of Finance	Tax Authority	Customs Authority	Public Procurement Agency	Ministry of Economic Planning (or equivalent)
23.a	Does the ministry/agency have an official email system?	E-mail					
23.b	Do the majority of the ministry's/agency's employees use the official email system?						
24	Does the ministry/agency have an internal knowledge platform (that is, intranet) used for the exchange of information and available only to staff?	Intranet					

(continues on next page)

CFA Questionnaire *(continued)*

Additional ministries/agencies:			Ministry/ agency 6	Ministry/ agency 7	Ministry/ agency 8	Ministry/ agency 9	Ministry/ agency 10
			Name:	Name:	Name:	Name:	Name:
23.a	Does the ministry/agency have an official email system?	E-mail					
23.b	Do the majority of the ministry's/agency's employees use the official email system?						
24	Does the ministry/ agency have an internal knowledge platform (that is, intranet) used for the exchange of information and available only to staff?	Intranet					

Note

1. It should be emphasized that low scores are not necessarily superior to high scores. In some cases, for example, tax collection, treasury functions and public procurement, greater devolution of functions is regarded as good practice, especially in countries which have reasonably strong institutions, and adequate human resource capacity.

Summary of CFA Case Studies

Benin

Region: AFR

Dates of CFA Mission: January 17–28, 2011

Mission team: Blanca Moreno-Dodson (Lead Economist); Emmanuel Bor (UNDP); Rethice Dagba (Local Consultant); John Heilbrunn (Political Economy Consultant); Lydia Montalti (Institutional and Human Resource Management Consultant); Maximilien Queyranne (Public Finance Specialist); Robert Yungu (Public Sector Specialist).

Main topics covered by the mission:

(1) Description of CFAs and their functions
(2) Macroeconomic and fiscal management
(3) *Preparation, execution,* and control of the budget in the West African Economic and Monetary Union (WAEMU)
(4) Analysis of PFM system: institutional and human resource inefficiencies
(5) Strategy for CFA reform in the WAEMU context.

Characteristics of the CFAs:

Relatively new democratic country with a strong presidential system and most CFA functions heavily centralized at the Ministry of Finance; limited decision-making power in the other agencies, as well as weak role of Parliament and control institutions; open civil society and press but with little influential role on public finance; endemic institutional and human resource inefficiencies due to lack of capabilities; clientelism and lack of budget transparency.

Main findings of the study:

Despite macroeconomic, fiscal stability, and PFM improvements over the last two decades, Benin CFAs are characterized by heavy centralization of public finance functions in the MoF, while the role of agencies at sectoral and subnational government levels remains very limited. Medium-term budget planning functions, including sector strategies, remain indicative but not binding. In addition, the role of Parliament and audit/control agency (*Court de Comptes*) remains very weak, with little influence on budget-related final decisions. Finally, current PFM practices lack consistency with regional UEMOA requirements. While institutional and human resources deficiencies are responsible for some of these systemic problems, lack of political will underlies the lack of progress and even worsening of PFM practices in recent years.

Cameroon

Region: AFR
Dates of CFA mission: February 7–24, 2011
Mission team: Verena Fritz (Governance Specialist), Zachary Mills (Public Finance Consultant); the mission was in the field jointly with an operational supervision mission led by Mamadou Deme (Senior Public Sector Specialist) and including Anand Rajaram (Sector Manager)

Main topics covered by the mission:

(1) CFA internal capabilities
(2) Four key interfaces (political level, line ministries, external partners, civil society)
(3) Program budgeting reform and the Nouveau Regime Financier (NRF)
(4) Public investment management.

Characteristics of CFAs:

As in many low-income countries, CFA functions in Cameroon are divided between a Ministry of Finance (MINFI) and a Ministry of Economic Affairs, Planning and Regional Development (MINEPAT). MINEPAT's main budget-related responsibility is for public investment preparation and selection in collaboration with line ministries. The two ministries had been merged for some time during the HIPC completion process, but were redivided after the completion point was reached. The Ministry of Finance is the largest among the ten countries included in the study with a total of over 12,000 staff (including tax and customs). MINEPAT is a smaller ministry with 900 staff. There are important challenges in terms strengthening staff skills and managing staff and change process.

Main findings of the study:

Cameroon's country and governance context is marked by hierarchy and relative inertia. This makes effective change management as needed for the PFM reforms under way challenging. On the positive side, government has made firm commitments to improve infrastructure and has bound itself to a schedule for the full implementation of the NRF by January 1, 2013. Consequently, there is an impetus for reforms and for improving CFA capabilities. Macro-fiscal management has been prudent, but no formal rules limiting budget deficits exist, and there are risks for the continuation of such a stance. The quality of PFM systems is still low on many dimensions, including budget credibility and accounting and reporting systems. While public investments have become a high political priority, the technical and political capacity to make good investment choices requires greater attention. Some innovative approaches for involving civil society in local public investment execution have been introduced. MTEF and program budgeting reforms take place on separate tracks (and split between the two CFAs) rather than being part of a more unified reform approach.

Chad

Region: AFR
Dates of CFA mission: December 1–14, 2010
Mission team: Emmanuel Pinto Moreira (Senior Economist), Gisèle Suire (Consultant), Guealbaye Manasset (Local Consultant)

Main topics covered by the mission:

(1) Mapping and evaluation of central finance functions
(2) Analysis of staffing and ICT issues in the finance ministry.

Characteristics of CFAs:

High fragmentation of central finance functions; scarce ICT support to the central finance functions; and deficient human resource management.

Main findings of the study:

The mission acknowledged the substantial progress accomplished after the start of the Action Plan for the Public Finance Modernization (PAMFIP). Nonetheless, numerous constraints still affect PFM performance. In particular, multiple institutions are responsible for functions that are typically carried out by the finance ministry. Such fragmentation led to a multiplication of structures and centers for decision making. In general, complex and frequently changing organizational structures mitigate against efforts to modernize CFAs and PFM systems. The human resources management of the finance ministry is weak and performance management is totally absent.

To address such deficiencies, the mission looked at possible ways to strengthen the organizational and administrative structure of the central finance ministry. Specific proposals include the establishment of a more stable internal organization and a clearer definition of the actors, procedures and responsibilities. ICT systems are also required and stable supply of electricity as well as reliable maintenance and transport systems have to be guaranteed. Finally, special attention should be paid toward strengthening recruitment and human resources management within the finance ministry.

Ghana

Region: AFR
Dates of CFA mission: May 25 to June 7, 2010
Mission team: Richard Allen (Consultant), Janet Piller (Senior Resource Manager), Nicholas Howard (Consultant), Sam Mensah (Consultant) and Fritz Gockel (Consultant).

Main topics covered by the mission:

(1) Description and analysis of CFA functions in Ghana
(2) Functional and organizational analysis of the finance ministry (MoFEP)
(3) Analysis of staffing and other HR issues in MoFEP.

Characteristics of CFAs:

Powerful but fragmented executive; finance and planning functions centralized in MoFEP; relatively strong parliament and little role for civil society; relatively open media reporting of budgetary and fiscal issues; underdeveloped use of ICT systems to broaden understanding of budgetary and fiscal issues.

Main findings of the study:

The Ministry of Finance and Economic Planning (MoFEP) has a generally solid organizational structure and has reasonably high capabilities in relation to countries of a similar size and level of development. A consulting group (ACET) is engaged in a business process review of the central departments and units of MoFEP, and worked closely with the CFA mission team during its visit. Several issues in MoFEP's organization and management were identified as problematic. It recommends that the ACET review be widened to cover the Controller and Auditor General's Department (CAGD), which employs over 3,000 accountants at all levels of government, and is of critical importance to the successful implementation of many government reforms, including the IFMIS project and the decentralization initiative. The report also recommends that the incentives and pay structures of economists and other key groups be reviewed in order to improve the ability of MoFEP to recruit and retain such staff in face of stiff competition from the Bank of Ghana and the private sector.

The report recommends that MoFEP's top management establish a high-level committee to oversee the program of work to strengthen MoFEP's capabilities. Management is encouraged to hire professionals in HR systems, business processes and change management from outside government to help in the process of implementation; and to engage MoFEP staff at all levels through consultation groups and other fora to help build a consensus both on the need for reform and the modalities of its implementation.

Mongolia

Region: EAP
Dates of CFA mission: May 2010
Mission team: Jim Brumby (Sector Manager), Zahid Hasnain (Senior Public Sector Specialist), Jonathan Dunn (Consultant), Maks Kobonbaev (Consultant) and Bertha Njembo (Consultant)

Main topics covered by the mission:

(1) Mapping and evaluationof central finance functions
(2) Capacity of the Ministry of Finance.

Characteristics of CFAs:

Most central finance functions executed by the Ministry of Finance; roles and responsibilities not clearly defined, in particular between the Ministry of Finance and the National Development and Innovation Committee (NDIC), which is responsible for planning; a high degree of political intervention in CFA processes, marked by very activist Parliament.

Main findings of the study:

The mission recognized recent progress towards macroeconomic stability and strengthening of Mongolian public financial management framework. However, it noted that Mongolian authorities still face significant challenges to responsible stewardship of natural resource rents as well as tradeoffs between short-term benefits of public expenditure and medium-term financial planning for equitable growth. A principal reform achievement in this area was the passage of the Fiscal Stability Law (FSL), aimed at promoting aggregate fiscal sustainability. Despite recent improvements, Mongolia demonstrates notable weaknesses in public procurement practices and public investment management, with generally weaker *de facto* than *de jure* performance. Both formal and informal political intervention in resource allocation decisions at central finance agencies is pervasive, eroding the ability of the Ministry of Finance to control its processes.

The mission suggested improvements in upstream and downstream aspects of PFM. Recommendations focused on addressing some uncertainties about the role of the NDIC, use of a multiyear project management system (such as a Public Investment Program), working of procurement processes, management of PPPs and some changes in the direction setting and management apparatus at the Ministry of Finance. The implementation of the FSL (slated for 2013) will be helpful to building the institutional framework for effective intertemporal fiscal management.

Nicaragua

Region: LAC
Dates of CFA mission: December 6–21, 2010
Mission team: Fernando Rojas (Consultant), Adrian Poffley (Chief Administrative Officer), and Francesco Grigoli (Consultant)

Main topics covered by the mission:

(1)   Description of the PFM Modernization Project
(2)   Assessment and gap analysis of the investment cycle
(3)   Proposals for a new public investment system.

Characteristics of CFAs:

Strong presidential system; limited role of the Ministry of Finance and Public Credit (MHCP) in public investment management; central finance functions highly fragmented and mainly distributed between the Presidency and MHCP.

Main findings of the study:

The current investment system is jointly financed by the government and external donors. There is acknowledgement within MHCP that the current investment system, whilst exhibiting some desirable features, is fragmented and inefficient. More specifically, there is only a weak connection between the investment proposals and the country's development priorities; limited coordination between the various players within government; evidence of divergent goals and inefficient resource allocation; an insufficiently clear mandate of the units responsible for planning, budgeting, and public investment units; and insufficient attention to critical phases of the project cycle such as planning and prioritization of investment goals, as well as the utilization, registration, maintenance, impact evaluation and renewal of capital assets.

In order to address these problems, the mission suggested developing a performance framework within which to manage public expenditure including investment; establishing stakeholder forums for dialogue on evaluation results and future priorities; and including an overall investment strategy in the National Development Plan, with links to the PFM Modernization Project. Moreover, steps need to be taken to disaggregate government priorities into public investment policies that can be cascaded down to sectors and individual government agencies. The political strength of the Presidency could be used to stimulate higher-quality ministerial goals and accountability for performance. Special attention should be paid to synchronizing public investment and budget processes within a multiyear perspective, to establishing a registry of new assets and to introducing a system for the ex-post evaluation of investments.

Rwanda

Region: AFR
Dates of CFA mission: November 9–22, 2010
Mission team: Richard Allen (Consultant), Janet Piller (Senior Resource Manager), Lewis Kabayiza Murara (Public Sector Specialist), and Francis Mugisha (Local Consultant).

Main topics covered by the mission:

(1) Description and analysis of CFA functions in Rwanda
(2) Functional and organizational analysis of the finance ministry (MINECOFIN)
(3) Analysis of staffing and other HR issues in MINECOFIN.

Characteristics of CFAs:

Strong presidential system; finance and planning functions centralized in the Ministry of Finance and Economic Planning (MINECOFIN); dominant executive, with relatively limited role for parliament and civil society; quite open media reporting of budgetary and fiscal issues.

Main findings of the study:

Public finance functions in Rwanda are heavily concentrated in the hands of MINECOFIN and the agencies that it supervises. MINECOFIN is one of the more powerful finance ministries in the region. Reforms of the Rwandan public service in recent years have focused on creating exceptionally lean organizational structures in central ministries and agencies (only c.500 staff in all central government agencies), combined with decentralization of service delivery and outsourcing of noncore functions. Further improvements are necessary to strengthen the capacity and capability of MINECOFIN and its agencies, especially in the fields of macroeconomic analysis and forecasting, debt management, the linkages between national development planning and the budget process ("shrinking the P"), tax policy, accounting and treasury functions, and public procurement.

To address high rates of staff turnover and weak staff incentives, MINECOFIN could consider developing a comprehensive medium-term strategy for building capacity, and attracting and retaining staff at both the entry and middle-management levels. Steps could also be taken to reduce the flatness of the existing grade structure, attract talented young professionals through a fast track program, introduce a new intermediate-level certification scheme for government accountants and financial managers, and encourage senior managers to participate in leadership and management training.

Sierra Leone

Region: AFR
Dates of CFA mission: October 2009; follow-up mission September 2010.
Mission team: Jim Brumby (Sector Manager), Vivek Srivastava (Senior Public Sector Specialist), Gibril Sesay and Murray Petrie (Consultants).

Main topics covered by the mission:

(1) Description and analysis of organizational structure of the Ministry of Finance and Economic Development (MOFED)
(2) Assessment of operating environment of CFAs
(3) Presentation of data and analysis of CFA functionality, and how CFA capability can be increased.

Characteristics of CFAs:

Strong technocratic leadership from MOFED, well supported at highest levels of government, gives the Ministry a degree of legitimacy and authority; MOFED is well structured but lacks capacity for effective decision making in key finance areas; donor support for PFM/CFA reform is not well coordinated, and there are serious political economy impediments to reform.

Main findings of the study:

From the very low point at the end of the civil war in 2002, Sierra Leone has achieved considerable progress in strengthening its institutions and PFM systems, and now rates close to the average for countries in the region.

The report recommends actions to strengthen the demand side for PFM reform (for example, promoting fiscal transparency as a general strategy and using the Parliament's Public Accounts Committee and civil society as champions); strengthening key watch-dog and sanctioning mechanisms (for example, the Anti-Corruption Commission); building presidential support for reform (for example, by linking CFA reform strategies to the PRSP-II and strengthening links between MOFED and the Strategic Policy Unit of the President); strengthening the management of MOFED and integrating Local Technical Assistants into the regular staff; building technical capacity in MOFED in areas such as revenue and tax policy, cash forecasting and cash management, internal audit, payroll management and procurement, public investment management, and enforcement of public finance laws; and strengthening donor coordination, the predictability of donor aid disbursements and their reporting of actual donor spending.

Tonga

Region: EAP
Dates of CFA mission: November 9–12, 2010
Mission team: Björn Dressel (consultant)

Outputs of mission:

(1) Report "Strengthening a Central Finance Agency in Times of Change: A Political Economy Study of Tonga's Ministry of Finance and National Planning", January 2011;
(2) CFA Questionnaire.

Main topics covered by the mission:

(1) Political economy analysis of the governance context in Tonga
(2) Functional and organizational analysis of the Ministry of Finance and National Planning (MOFNP), including key external relationships
(3) Evaluation of the reform context and development strategy.

Characteristics of CFAs:

Neo-patrimonial, hybrid governance system; finance and planning functions centralized in MOFNP; dominant executive, with weak parliament and little role for civil society; open, yet limited, media reporting of budgetary and fiscal issues.

Main findings of the study:

Public finance functions in Tonga are traditionally concentrated in the hands of MOFNP. As a relatively lean (that is, a staff of about 130) and high-skilled organization, MOFNP occupies a central role in managing public finances, and has led a successful reform of the PFM system over the last decade. Yet, recent developments have also illustrated a declining lead role of the MOFNP, partly as a result of growing assertiveness of political actors and organizational fragmentation (that is, creation of a separate Ministry of Revenue), partly due to capability issues at the helm of MOFNP itself. Further improvements are necessary to strengthen the capability of the ministry and its units, especially in the fields of macroeconomic analysis and forecasting, treasury and cash flow management, financial reporting, as well as reinforcing linkages with external actors such as the audit office, civil society and donor community.

In light of major constitutional and political changes, MOFNP should consider undertaking a comprehensive review of core business processes to clarify the status and strategic direction of reform and maximize the value of technical assistance. MOFNP could also consider developing a comprehensive medium-term strategy for building capacity, and attracting and retaining staff at both the entry and middle-management levels. Finally, steps should also be taken to establish more formal interaction with parliament and civil society through regular consultation, sharing of financial analysis and information, and lending support to a financial framework law.

Republic of Yemen

Region: MENA
Dates of CFA mission: July 23 to August 7, 2010
Mission team: Richard Allen (Consultant), Adrian Poffley (Chief Administrative Officer), and Francesco Grigoli (Consultant)

Main topics covered by the mission:

(1) Map and analysis of the central finance functions;
(2) Review of the functions where the Ministry of Finance (MoF) and the Ministry of Planning and International Cooperation (MoPIC) interface or overlap;
(3) Assessment of the MoF's organizational structure, staffing and HR management systems.

Characteristics of CFAs:

Strong presidential system; relatively decentralized central finance functions; poor coordination arrangements between MoF and MoPIC on macroeconomic forecasting, budget preparation and development planning; considerable scope for strengthening organizational structure, HR management, ICT systems, and internal coordination of the MoF.

Main findings of the study:

The allocation of core finance functions is not well designed in the Republic of Yemen. Responsibility for macroeconomic analysis and forecasting is divided among MoPIC and several other agencies and is poorly coordinated. There is no single, dedicated unit within the MoF (or MoPIC) that is responsible for undertaking analytical work on expenditure policy and tax policy issues; and no medium- and long-term strategy for managing government debt. Treasury functions are mainly carried out by the Central Bank of the Republic of Yemen. Incentives are not oriented towards encouraging or rewarding high performance, and the proliferation of government committees warrants the payment of bonuses for routine work.

To address these problems, the mission suggested a restructuring of MoF in the long term into a significantly smaller, policy-oriented organization with high-caliber staff and a mandate focused on macroeconomic and fiscal policy. In the short term a reconsideration of the respective roles of the MoF and MoPIC and a consolidation of the treasury functions into the MoF is required. Moreover, strengthening interministerial cooperation on the setting of priorities through the budget and national development plan, as well as macroeconomic forecasting, is critical. The mission recommended that a review of the core business processes in MoF be undertaken, with a view to increasing the efficiency of the ministry's operations and decision-making processes; investing in top talent to strengthen the skills-base of the MoF; and developing HR policies and practices that support a high performance culture.

Environmental Benefits Statement